MAX ALLEN

**photographs by
ADRIAN LANDER**

SNIFF
SWIRL&
SLURP

how to get more pleasure out of every glass of wine

MITCHELL BEAZLEY

Sniff Swirl & Slurp

by Max Allen

First published in Great Britain in 2002 by
Mitchell Beazley, an imprint of Octopus Publishing
Group Limited, 2–4 Heron Quays, London E14 4JP.

A CIP catalogue record for this book is available from
the British Library.

ISBN: 1 84000 513 0

Photographs by Adrian Lander

Commissioning Editors: Rebecca Spry, Hilary Lumsden
Executive Art Editor: Yasia Williams
Managing Editor: Emma Rice
Designer: Geoff Borin
Editor: Jamie Ambrose

Typeset in Frutiger

Printed and bound in China

CONTENTS

INTRODUCTION

This is not a book about tasting wine; it's a book about *drinking* wine. That may seem like a subtle difference to you, but it's a fundamental difference to me. Tasting wine can be hard work; drinking wine is fun. And I don't know about you, but I'd much rather have fun than work.

I spend a large part of almost every day tasting wine. I write about it, review it, talk about it, judge it at wine competitions, teach other people how to taste it and appreciate it, and even occasionally help to make it. But the more I taste wine – scrutinizing its colour, taking thoughtful sniffs, sipping carefully, swirling the liquid around my mouth as I ponder its subtleties, then usually spitting it out and scribbling down some bogus tasting note – the more I think that I'm missing the point. Oh, sure: tasting carefully is the only way to learn about wine, about its differences in flavour, its regional characteristics, its styles, its quirks. But the only way to really understand wine is to drink it: with food, with friends, with music, with laughter – without, in fact, thinking too hard about it. Not that I am advocating a less precious approach to wine.

After all, for most of us (even wine nerds like me, whose idea of a scintillating bedtime read is the latest wine atlas of Germany), wine is a pleasurable part of life: like music, food, clothes, going out. It's not something separate, academic, dry, and "out there". It's in here: on my table, threatening to be knocked over by rioting kids; in plastic cups at a barbecue; in the finest crystal by candlelight if I'm feeling incurably romantic; being sluiced over some steak for a quick marinade; being given as a gift to someone I love.

So, yes: this is yet another book about wine appreciation, but it's also a book about appreciation through loud, joyous drinking rather than quiet, contemplative tasting.

HOW THE BOOK WORKS

Most wine books are admirably logical in their approach. They will tell you – in a clearly constructed, chronological, carefully delineated way – about the various elements of wine, starting with descriptions of the grape varieties, then what happens in the vineyard, then about the wine regions of the world, then about serving and storing, etc., etc. The idea is that, by the end of the book, the reader knows more about the nuts and bolts of wine and is therefore able (theoretically) to get more pleasure out of it.

I've written books like that before, but I don't feel admirably logical this time around. In this book, I'm heading for the same destination, but I'm taking an alternative route.

I've approached the topic by imagining you, the consumer, standing in a wine shop, thinking about what you want to drink with tonight's dinner. You've probably got a whole load of not particularly chronological questions running through your head. What do the different grape varieties taste like? If I spend more money, am I going to get a better wine? What's the difference between a Chardonnay from here and Chardonnay from there? What makes a biodynamic wine so special? Why are full-bodied, alcoholic red wines so popular? What are the best wines to buy for a party? I wonder if I can get the cute assistant manager's phone number?

Each of the chapters in this book, then, represents an answer to one of those questions (except for the one about the phone number). I've tried to illustrate each answer by "opening" a bundle of wines, describing them as if we were drinking them together, and explaining all the aspects of wine relevant to that answer. So in each chapter, details of winemaking techniques sit next to wine-and-food matching suggestions; these come before opinionated rants on our changing wine culture, which in turn relate to descriptions of the various wines I've chosen to illustrate that chapter's theme, and so on.

The chapters aren't meant to be a series of academic exercises; they're meant to be as they're written: enthusiastic, personal, themed wine raves, with some educational stuff thrown in for good measure. If you want to try and replicate them at home, by going out and buying examples of the wines mentioned, bringing them home, and trying to find in your glass what I write about on the page, then that's great.

But quite honestly, I don't expect you to do that. Instead, what I hope this book will do is at least inspire you to go out, buy a couple of different bottles of any good wine, bring them home, cook up a meal, invite your mates round, open the bottles, drink, compare their contents, and have such a good time that you'll want to do it all again. And again.

Because that's the point: you only really understand when you get obsessed.

Max Allen

TOOLS OF THE TRADE

The things you need to get more pleasure out of wine

Most of the guff and nonsense surrounding wine – the jargon, the accessories, the rituals – can seem intimidating to beginners. But I'm warning you right now: once you start falling for wine's charms, you'll find yourself turning into yet another jargon/accessory/ritual junkie.

You see, wine is just like any other passion: when you get into it, you've just *got* to get the right gear. Imagine a passionate cook without good knives; a passionate musician without a good instrument; a passionate tech-head without the latest gadgets and games. Wine's no different. Once you're hooked, you'll find yourself spending a lot of time and money in wine-accessory shops (and, hopefully, book shops). Your old non-winey friends might take a little time adjusting to the new, claret-soaked you. They might laugh at your sniffing and swirling and slurping – not to mention your fascination with antique decanters. But they'll soon come round when they twig that you're drinking better wine than they are.

As well as spending more money on wine accessories, you'll also find that you'll be spending more money on wine itself, as you become wrapped up in its spell. It's just a fact of getting into wine, I'm afraid: the more good wine you drink, the more you want to drink good wine. And good wine tends to be more expensive than bad wine (*see* the chapter on "Posh Wines", page 84, for more on this).

So I reckon that you owe it to yourself to do whatever you can to maximize your wine enjoyment – to maximize the return on your investment, if you want to see it that way – by getting some good wine-drinking equipment, and learning "The Clever Wine-Drinker's Ritual", page 11. Believe me: these things make a difference.

THE EQUIPMENT

Of course, you don't need all the fancy equipment – the decanter, the posh French wine thermometer, the industrial-strength bottle opener, the latest Austrian stemware. There are only two things you really need to drink wine: an efficient corkscrew and a simple glass. But we all know there's a big difference between need and want.

I have a shed full of fancy glasses, antique corkscrews, and obscure traditional European tasting vessels, all gathering dust. But I constantly fall back on just three basic tools.

For everyday tasting and drinking, I use what's called the International Organization for Standards (ISO) tasting glass, which has all the right attributes: it's clear, it has a stem (so my hand doesn't warm the wine), and the bowl of the glass converges toward the rim, concentrating the wine's smells toward my nose. All other good glasses, regardless of size and price, should at least have these qualities, but I keeping returning to the ISOs because they're cheap (which means I'm prepared if a gang of thirsty people turn up unannounced), they go in the dishwasher (*very* important), and they're easily replaceable (I don't know about you, but the more precious the glass, the more likely I am to break it).

For opening my bottles, I use whichever waiter's friend-type corkscrew I can find at the back of the cutlery drawer when I get the urge to open a bottle. The only thing I really care about in a corkscrew is whether the screw itself is the proper coil shape, so it can get a good grip on the cork. Antique corkscrews look lovely, but they're not always practical. The Teflon-coated, lever-model, lifetime-guarantee corkscrews are great – but by crikey, they're expensive.

And my third trusty item of paraphernalia is an old Italian ceramic wine jug. Glass decanters can be beautiful things – especially the really wide ones that you can swirl your Cabernet around in, watching the garnet-coloured liquid pick up flashes of candlelight. Yet for practical reasons, I prefer my jug: I usually pour the decanted wine back in the bottle before putting it on the table, so presentation's not all that important (*see* "Tall, Dark, & Handsome", page 74, for more info on decanting).

However, just because I've pared my wine accessory range down to a bare minimum, that doesn't mean you shouldn't go right ahead and splurge on that posh French wine thermometer, the Austrian stemware....

THE CLEVER WINE-DRINKER'S RITUAL

This is perhaps the most important part of the whole book. I want you to get into the habit of spending just a few seconds going through this simple but highly enjoyable ritual each time you try a new glass of wine. You may feel a little awkward at first, but you'll soon get the hang of the process and end up doing it naturally.

First, don't pour your glass too full – about half-full is good. You're going to be swirling the wine and sticking your nose in the glass, so you need a bit of space.

Now look carefully at the wine if you've got enough light (most of your wine drinking will probably be done in romantically dim surroundings, so don't worry too much about this). Check out the wine's clarity and its colour; I'll go into more details about what you're looking for when describing each of the wines through the book.

Give the glass a quick swirl to release the wine's aromas, then stick your nose in and take a good sniff. Get a "smell-snapshot" of the wine fixed in your mind. Then pour some of the wine into your mouth (less than the generous gulps you'll be helping yourself to in a minute, but more than a genteel sip). Sloosh the wine around to every corner of your gums, thinking about how it feels on your tongue, whether it tastes like it smells. And then swallow it, checking out whether and how the wine lingers at the back of your throat. (If you're trying lots of wines at once, you might want to spit the wine out rather than swallow it, just to keep yourself nice, and your head clear for as long as possible. Otherwise, I'm a big advocate of swallowing.)

You might want to repeat the process quickly – usually if the wine is either really bad (to check what's wrong with it) or really good (to appreciate all its subtleties) – but then I'd just go back to ordinary drinking, occasionally perhaps swirling, sniffing, and slurping to see how the wine's "travelling" as it sits in your glass. Because it will change as it warms up (or cools down) and reacts with the air you're introducing it to with each swirl. Hopefully that change will be for the better – every time you take a sniff or a slurp, the wine will offer a new nuance.

See? How easy is that? Please, do try this ritual at home: it will add immeasurably to your enjoyment of wine. Make a habit of it and you won't need books like this. You'll learn everything you need to know about wine just by drinking it.

IT'S ALL ABOUT FLAVOUR

How different grape varieties make different styles of wine

It's important to understand that flavour and taste are not the same thing. In most western cultures, at least, the words "taste" and "flavour" have become interchangeable, but in fact they are different, although linked, processes. Let me explain what I'm talking about here, by way of a little story about flu.

I had a shocking dose of the flu recently. You know: one of those crippling colds that you should stay in bed for a week to get over, but you never do, so it takes twice as long to shake. As well as the aches and pains, sore throat and nausea, though, the most crippling aspect of the affliction was that it completely blocked my nostrils for a fortnight. For two long weeks – fourteen interminable, flavourless days – I could smell nothing. Absolutely nothing. Which meant, of course, that there was no point in drinking wine: yes, the alcohol is nice, and the cool fizz of a glass of Champagne, for example, is refreshing, but it's the smell and flavour of wine that gives me the most pleasure.

HOW WE TASTE AND SMELL WINE

We taste in the mouth, through tiny sensors on our tongue and gums. These sensors physically register acidity, sugar, bitterness, and saltiness. Despite what we say ("I can't taste a bloody thing – aaaCHOO!"), we *can* still taste when our noses are blocked up by the flu. Which means that we can still tell the difference between sweetness, saltiness, etc.

Smell and flavour, on the other hand, are picked up in a different way. When we smell, tiny particles of whatever it is we're smelling float up our nostrils and are registered by nerve endings in the deep, dark recesses of our sinuses. These messages are transmitted to the primordial part of our brains that match up the smell to memories of the last time we experienced the smell, or to other memories associated with that experience. This is why drinking wine can sometimes border on the mystical – why the fact that simple, fermented grape juice can evoke sometimes painfully emotional memories strikes me as magical.

"Flavour" is the word we use to describe the process of smelling from the inside, when particles of the wine in our mouths are forced up the nasal passages at the back of the throat towards the same nerve endings that registered the smell of the wine from the outside. This is why, when your nasal and sinus cavities are blocked by a cold or the flu (or a particularly vicious hangover), your sense of smell (and flavour) is lost. And drinking wine is almost pointless.

HOW GRAPE VARIETIES AFFECT FLAVOUR

Of all the countless factors that make one wine's flavours different from those of another, the grape variety (or varieties) used is arguably the most important. Just as there are different varieties of apples with distinct colours, textures, and flavours, so there are different varieties of grape vines, each with distinct characteristics. Each grape variety has crucially different flavour compounds in its pulp and its skin, producing different flavours in the finished wine.

Importantly, though, while some varieties produce wines that are worlds apart in style, others produce wines that can have a family resemblance. Recognizing the differences and similarities of the flavours of grape varieties is the key to understanding wine, learning about your personal preferences, and trying out new grape varieties with confidence. If you like the dark, blackberry flavours of red wine produced from Merlot, for example, then you'll probably also like the similar-tasting wines produced from Cabernet Franc, but you might not like the paler, spicier, stronger wines produced from Grenache.

A ROSE BY ANY OTHER NAME

While you may think that the flavour descriptions used by wine writers like me are way over the top ("the wine has an entrancing bouquet of garlands of wild flowers cascading down a Provençal hillside in early spring" etc., etc.), some of the time we're more accurate than you might realize. Sauvignon Blanc, for example, doesn't just "smell like" cut grass; the aromatic molecules flooding into my nasal passages are actually the same pungent combination of chemicals (called methoxypyrazines, if you must know) as those you'll find in cut grass.

DRINKING IT

The wines we're going to drink in this chapter are all white wines. The first three – Riesling, Sauvignon Blanc, and Gewürztraminer – are also unwooded, aromatic wines, which means they are the product of quite distinct, strongly flavoured white grapes that have been simply fermented and bottled without any complicated, flavour-altering winemaking techniques. In other words, it should be easy to pick out the varietal flavour differences in these wines. At the very least, it should be fun trying. In the other chapters, I'll talk about food quite a lot, but for this first chapter I've decided to leave food references to a minimum, because it might confuse the issue a little.

WINE 1: RIESLING

You've just got to start a book on wine drinking with a nice, cold glass of young (say, one- or two-year-old) Riesling. Nothing in the whole world of wine comes closer to capturing the intense thrill of pure, varietal grape flavour – partly because of the Riesling grape variety's distinct characteristics, and partly because almost all Riesling is made so simply: the grapes are picked, crushed, fermented, and bottled – and that's about it. Pick up a glass of young Riesling and it'll even look pure: pale and clear, like spring water. It will smell like – well, it'll smell and taste like cold, freshly squeezed green grapes (and that, surprisingly, is one of the few times you'll read the word "grapes" as a tasting note in this book). It *should* taste like that, too: zingy, refreshing, with the thrill of citrus fruit, and a lingering but delicate flavour that hangs around at the back of the throat.

WINE 2: SAUVIGNON BLANC

Compare the Riesling you've just tried to a young, New World Sauvignon Blanc from, say, New Zealand. Although the glass of cold white wine has been made in an almost identical way (simply fermented grape juice) and looks nearly identical (almost water-pale) take one sniff of the Sauvignon and you'll find that it's quite different. Where the Riesling's aromas were intense but delicate, this Sauvignon's smells are full-on and pungent: there's gooseberry and passion-fruit, and maybe a sprinkling of fresh-mown grass. In the mouth, too, this wine is quite different; it's fuller-flavoured and more assertive, with a similar citric-acid freshness and zing, but broader and riper-tasting. And there you have it: the most important thing distinguishing this from the last wine we tasted is the grape variety that was used to make it. First lesson learned. You're halfway to becoming as wine-obsessed as I am.

WINE 3: GEWURZTRAMINER

EXAMPLES

Alsace (France)
Chile
New Zealand

If you haven't got the hang of this different grape variety game by now, then open a bottle of Gewürztaminer, arguably the most distinctive and recognizable white wine of them all, and let this wine slap you in the nostrils. Gewürz, as I like to call it (the word means "spicy" in German), is the variety that most often teaches wine newcomers about The Joy of the Poetic Tasting Note. When you smell a particularly aromatic Gewurz from Alsace (minus the ü), for example, it's really not too far-fetched to imagine you're sticking your nose into a glass full of rose petals steeped in lychee juice – even though the sensible part of you (the part that drinks light beer), knows you're smelling the product of fermented grapes. This is one reason why I love Gewürz: for its uncompromising varietal quality. The other is because, although it's a cliché to say so, its high-energy perfume and oily richness in the mouth are a perfect accompaniment to south-east Asian cooking (Thai, Vietnamese, Malaysian) – and I love south-east Asian food.

WINE 4: VIOGNIER

EXAMPLES

Condrieu (Rhône, France)
Australia
California
southern France

I once opened a bottle of Viognier, from the Languedoc region in the south of France, at a kid's birthday party (hey, just because *they're* drinking lemonade, doesn't mean *I* have to). It was a particularly varietal example – which means it strongly displayed all the flavour and taste characteristics I'd expect to find in a good Viognier. So I passed a glass round to some of the adults (and a couple of the kids) in the room and asked them what they could smell. And all of them (including the kids), took one sniff, looked at me incredulously, and, independently of each other, said, "Apricots." Which is pretty amazing, considering that not one of them would have read a wine book like this which could have told them that Viognier, when it's good, has the most amazing smell of dried apricots, an oily character like Gewürz, and the richness and softness of a good Chardonnay.

DRINKING TIP: DRINKING MORE WINES

This is going to sound terribly indulgent, I know, but can I suggest you get into the habit of having more than one bottle of wine open at a time when you sit down to eat? It's only by constantly comparing and contrasting wines made from different varieties, different regions, different producers – by putting each wine into context – that you'll develop a real understanding. Don't worry too much about them spoiling after you've opened them: stick the cork back in each bottle, keep the whites in the fridge, and they should drink well for a couple of days. They'll change over that time, too, as they react slowly with the air and oxidize – which can be a lesson in itself.

WINE 5: TREBBIANO

EXAMPLES

Bianco di Custoza, Frascati, Orvieto, Soave (Italy)

Whether it's called Trebbiano in Italy or Ugni Blanc in France, this grape variety is planted all over the place, but it seldom appears by name on the label. It is more likely to be found as a major component of a blend in the Italian white wines mentioned in the "where to find it" box to the left (*see* also "Fiddling Around", page 56, for more on blending). Despite being widely planted, though, Trebbiano is not known for its quality – or, in fact, its flavour. This is because it hasn't really got any: quality *or* flavour. Indeed, its tart, neutral blandness is this grape variety's only redeeming feature (that and the fact that when it's distilled, it makes good brandy, which accounts for there being so much of it in France).

But Trebbiano has a huge role to play in this chapter in showing you that not all grape varieties have overt flavours like Riesling or Viognier. And sometimes, in mid-summer, when you're eating seafood in a beach-side café, a cold, flavourless, not-terribly strong white wine drunk by the bucketful is just the ticket to quench your thirst. After all: there is a time and a place for everything.

THE MAINSTREAM GRAPES

There are thousands of different grape varieties in the world, but only a few dozen, like those mentioned in this chapter, are planted on a large scale. Here are some other top performers and brief descriptions of the wines they produce (you'll be introduced to these and other grapes elsewhere in the book, too).

WHITE WINES

CHARDONNAY

Do I really need to describe it? It yields almost every style of white wine, from crisp and bland to unctuous and exciting, and is made in every corner of the globe.

CHENIN BLANC

In France's Loire Valley particularly, Chenin is used to make all styles, from sparkling through bone-dry, long-lived whites to luscious, immortal, sweet whites.

SEMILLON

Often blended with Sauvignon Blanc to make full-bodied, oak-aged wines in Bordeaux; on its own makes long-lived, lemony whites in Australia. Also goes into good, honeyed sweet wines all over the world.

MUSCAT

The name "Muscat" belongs to a whole family of grapes, almost all of which are used to make sweet wines, from the sweet, frothy Moscato in Italy to the rich, syrupy, fortified Muscats of Australia.

RED WINES

CABERNET SAUVIGNON

Used to make dark, tannic, long-lived, full-bodied, blackcurranty red wines, whether grown in Bordeaux, California, or Australia, or elsewhere.

PINOT NOIR

Often pale-ish red wines, aromatic, cherry-like, lighter-bodied, but the best from Burgundy, America, New Zealand, and elsewhere can have more weight and amazing earthy complexity.

GRENACHE

Produces spicy, peppery, gamey, sometimes leathery and alcoholic red wines, originally from the southern Rhône Valley, and all across Spain and the Mediterranean. Also grown in Australia and elsewhere.

MERLOT

Grown all over the place – from Bordeaux to Italy to Washington State, the USA – Merlot produces sometimes leafy, but often plummy and plush red wines.

SYRAH OR SHIRAZ

Known as Syrah in France, where it tastes of spice, dried herbs, and liquorice; and Shiraz in Australia and other New World countries, where it is richer, more blackberry-like, and chocolatey.

SANGIOVESE

The main red grape of Chianti in Tuscany, but grown all over Italy (and Australia and the USA), producing dark, cherry- and almond-flavoured wines.

TEMPRANILLO

The great grape of northern Spain (most recognizably Rioja), yielding wines that seem to combine Pinot Noir's bright lightness with Merlot's dark fleshiness.

ZINFANDEL

The wild, spicy, forest-fruit-flavoured red grape of California (related to the Primitivo grape of southern Italy). Zin can make hugely alcoholic, rich, full-bodied reds.

TASTE THE EARTH

Wines that taste of where they're from

Wine's extraordinary ability to express a sense of place through its taste and flavour makes it universally and enduringly special to us humans. Think about it: someone plants a vine in some dirt, grows some grapes, picks them when they're ripe, crushes 'em, ferments the juice until it becomes wine, and then you drink it. If it's good, that wine can speak eloquently to you of all the sunshine and rain that fell on the vine's leaves; of the minerals and nutrients that were sucked up from the cool soil by the vine's roots; of the winemaker's care, attention, and knowledge as he or she crushed, plunged, racked, splashed, and bottled the wine into existence.

I opened a bottle of wine the other day. Nothing unusual about that. In fact, it'd be far more unusual if I said, "I didn't open a bottle of wine the other day", what with me being a wine writer and everything. Very unusual indeed. Downright bloody weird, in fact.

Anyway, I opened a bottle of wine the other day, a white wine, a blend of Semillon and Sauvignon Blanc grapes from the Margaret River region of Western Australia. I poured a glass and took a casual sniff – the way you do, you know, just to check it wasn't tainted or anything – and I was going to pass the bottle round to the other people in the room, standing there with their glasses empty, looking at me with thirsty eyes, when the smell from the wine registered in that primal bit of the brain that stores all your memories and... well, I'm not quite sure what happened next, but it was freaky.

WHEN A WINE "SPEAKS"

The room and my friends' faces went all blurry and I was transported straight to Margaret River in late summer. I could see the tall stands of majestic Karri gum trees; the lush, thick-trunked vineyards in their gravelly beds, fringed by ranks of more gums in full blossom. I could feel the warm, blue heat above me, and those beautiful, wafting Margaret River

breezes ruffling my shirt, bringing smells of hay and dry earth and sweet, salty sea air. I could see the surf crashing onto the sand at Prevelly Park beach. I could taste the rare-roasted, milk-fed lamb and local sheeps-milk cheeses, and I could hear the Margaret River Hotel band pumping on a Saturday night, mingling with the shouts and the laughter of the local surfies, cellar hands, tourists, and artists.

And then, clunk! I was back in a cold room in an outer suburb of a grey city, holding a heavy bottle of wine and a glass. So I poured myself another splash and, trembling, took a sip.

And stone me if it didn't happen again. Whack! One mouthful of this pale-green liquid with its utterly unmistakable herbaceous, zesty, gooseberry and passion-fruit flavours, and I was back again in Margaret River, eating prawn curry and drinking beer, staring up at the Milky Way later that night, listening to the surf far off in the distance....

As you can imagine, by the time we got to the end of the bottle, I was wading through a damp sense of longing, trying to work out how I could convince my family to move to Margaret River. All because of the smell and taste (and yes, OK: the alcohol) in some fermented grape juice.

TERMINOLOGY TIME: TERROIR

The French – as they would – have a word that encompasses wine's ability to absorb and then convey all the experiences of its environment, microclimate, and vinification techniques. That word is terroir. It translates roughly as "the vine's environment", but has connotations that extend right into the glass: in other words, if a wine tastes of somewhere, if the flavours distinctly make you think of a particular place on the surface of this globe, then that wine is expressing its terroir.

Of course, some wines are more eloquent than others. Particular grape varieties flourish in regions that are totally unsuited to other varieties. Pinot Noir, for example, is a red grape with relatively delicate flavours – flavours that a need long, cool growing season to develop. As a result, Pinot Noir doesn't tend to do well in hot regions with short growing seasons, conditions that are just right for Mourvèdre: a solid, brawny-tasting red grape variety that needs heaps of warmth in order to ripen properly.

Put another way, wines from different places speak in different languages, just as people do. And that is very much a part of the whole fun of drinking them (the wines, that is – not the people).

DRINKING IT

We're thinking global to start off with in this
chapter, comparing the same grape variety grown
at opposite ends of the earth; then we'll narrow
down the field to look at how the same grape
variety compares when grown in neighbouring
countries. Next, we'll look at how grapes grown on
one side of a hill can yield wine that tastes slightly
different to wine made from the same sort of grapes
grown on another side of the same hill. I know that
spotting such differences is one of the most easily
ridiculed aspects of wine tasting, but trust me: once
you've tasted those differences for yourself, you'll
have the last, delicious laugh.

WINE 1: FRENCH SAUVIGNON BLANC

EXAMPLES

Sancerre, Pouilly Fumé, Menetou-Salon (Loire, France)

Okay. You've opened a bottle of one- or two-year-old Sancerre. It's pale, almost water-white in the glass; looks safe enough. Then you take a sniff and your nose is assaulted – but not by the smell of fresh, ripe grapes, as you'd expect from this grape variety if you were with us in the last chapter. Instead, the smell contains minerals (such as powdered lime) and flowers as well as some gooseberry notes. Then you put it in your mouth and it tastes like stone and chalk and flowers, too. In other words, it tastes unmistakably like wine made from grapes grown in the limestone and flint soils of the region. Then again, look at the label: the words "Sauvignon Blanc" don't even rate a mention, while the word "Sancerre" is the most prominent feature. That's because in most traditional wine regions of the world, where wine comes from has always been more important than what it was made from.

When it comes down to it, this one is a bit of a chicken-and-egg argument, really: do wines styles develop in traditional regions to match the local food, or do regional foods develop to go with the local wines? The reality is probably going to be found somewhere in the middle. The same environmental factors that influence grape and wine flavour also influence the fruit, vegetables, and animals of the same region. As a result, it's no surprise that strictly regional food-and-wine matches tend to work really well.

The following examples show what I mean:

- ♉ Medium-dry Spanish amontillado sherry and Spanish ham
- ♉ Kangaroo and rich South Australian Shiraz
- ♉ Atlantic mussels and a crisp, dry Loire Valley white
- ♉ Coq au vin and a good red burgundy
- ♉ Roquefort cheese and Sauternes

I could go on and on. Good matches don't have to come from exactly the same place on the earth, though; in fact, sticking to only a vague regional theme can be a good inspiration when you're thinking about what to eat and drink. So the mussels may be from New Zealand and the crisp, dry white may be from South Africa; the blue cheese may be from Australia and the sweet white wine may be from Canada, but the matches are still going to be lovely.

Then, of course, there are those great food-and-wine matches that bring together almost diametrically opposed cultures and regions: bright German Riesling from the cold Mosel Valley and a fragrant fish curry from the sweltering beaches of Thailand, for example, or a heady, heavily spiced Moroccan lamb tagine with a rich Argentine Malbec. Yum and yum! These may blow my terroir theory out of the water, but they taste delicious – so who cares?

WINE 2: NEW WORLD SAUVIGNON BLANC

EXAMPLES

Adelaide Hills, Margaret River (Australia)

Hawke's Bay, Marlborough, Martinborough (New Zealand)

Chile

On the face of it, a glass of Chilean Sauvignon Blanc looks exactly like Sancerre: water-white, kind of innocuous. Take one sniff, though, and you'll see right away that these wines may be from the same family but they reside at different ends of the earth. There is more fruit to smell in the New World: lots of passion-fruit, gooseberry, and blackcurrant leaf, all typical Sauvignon characters. In the mouth, too, it's all sweet, pulpy, grapey flavours and crisp acidity – but hardly any of the chalk or minerals or flowers. This is due to many factors. For a start, the soils are quite different in Chile: less stony, more fertile. The grape yields are higher; there is more sunshine producing riper, fruitier flavours. And while Sauvignon has been grown in Sancerre for hundreds of years, many of the vineyards in Chile (and most of the vineyards in places like New Zealand) are relative newcomers, with perhaps only thirty years' history. As a result, the variety takes precedence over the region on the label.

WINE 3: ITALIAN PINOT GRIGIO

EXAMPLES

Friuli, Trentino (Italy)

Pinot Grigio was such a popular restaurant wine throughout the 1990s that you've probably already drunk loads of it without even realizing. That crisp, almost neutral, maybe slightly melon-flavoured white you like at your local pizza place? Probably a Pinot Grigio. The reason is that in regions like Friuli, in north-east Italy, the Pinot Grigio grape, grown in the cool, sometimes steep hillside vineyards, produces the kind of light, easy-to-understand, not terribly challenging, unwooded, dry white wine that "goes" with almost anything: whether you're drinking fish or pasta, whether you're out to dinner with your boss, your mother-in-law, your kids, whatever. Funny thing is, it's a brown-skinned cousin of the red grape, Pinot Noir – even though it produces very pale, almost green-tinged white wine.

THE GLOBALIZATION OF WINE

For a while there, about a decade ago, in fact, "Flying Winemakers" (often Australian-trained) were all the rage. Sent into "traditional" winemaking countries such as the south of France and Eastern Europe to make cheap wine for supermarkets, these young global *vignerons* set about planting Chardonnay and Cabernet and cleaning up the wineries. Critics wailed that this "McDonald's approach" would lead to a worrying standardization – that in each country, wine's essential "somewhereness" would be sacrificed in favour of consistency and familiarity. While this has happened to a certain extent – mostly at the bottom end of the market – I actually reckon that exposure to the diversity of traditional winemaking has led to a resurgence of interest in distinctly regional wines among younger winemakers. And this has to be A Good Thing.

WINE 4: FRENCH PINOT GRIS

WHAT TO LOOK FOR

Pinot Gris does crop up in other parts of France, but its home is in Alsace, on the country's western border with Germany

Pinot Gris is the French name for Pinot Grigio (both *grigio* and *gris* mean "grey" – but you knew that). Look at Pinot Gris grapes growing on a vine in Alsace and they look almost identical to Pinot Grigio grapes growing on a vine in Friuli – or Oregon (the USA), New Zealand, or Australia. But taste an Alsace Pinot Gris, and it could have been made from a different grape variety altogether. It's fuller in every sense, from the floral smells to the fat, oily, even luscious texture and higher alcohol (Grigio is seldom more than about twelve per cent alcohol, while Gris can often be around fourteen per cent in a warm year). The difference, of course, comes almost solely from the terroir: Alsace's vineyards are surprisingly sunny and planted in different soils to those of north-east Italy.

NATIONALISM IN A GLASS

Some grape varieties have become strongly associated with certain spots on the globe, and are seldom found elsewhere – or certainly not in a similar style. White-wine examples include light, lemony, unwooded Semillon from the Hunter Valley in Australia, and aromatic, racy Albariño in the wines of Rías Baixas in Galicia, north-west Spain. On the red side, there is the funky, wild-berry-tasting Zinfandel from California, and the vivid, bright, liqueured-cherry-flavoured Pinotage of South Africa.

APPELLATION CONTROL

Many countries – particularly those in the so-called "Old World" (France, Italy, Spain, Germany, etc.) place so much importance on wine's "somewhereness" that they codify in law what each wine-grower is allowed (and not allowed) to do in order to put the regional designation on his or her label. In France, the *appellation contrôlée* (AC or AOC) system proscribes grape varieties, maximum yields, and winemaking methods. In Italy a similar system exists called *Denominazione di Origine Controllata* (DOC); in Spain, it's *Denominación de Origen* (DO), and so on.

In newer wine-producing countries, where such laws are seen as affronts to the very basic human rights of every winemaker, appellation systems tend to limit themselves simply to marking boundaries. So where a wine from France with an *appellation contrôlée* name on it indicates that it should taste like wine from that region, an Australian wine with a regional name on it indicates only that the wine was made from fruit grown within that region's boundary – although it'll probably have just as much regional character as the French wine, in its own unique way.

WINE 5 & WINE 6: TWO DIFFERENT CRU BEAUJOLAIS

EXAMPLES

pick from any of the ten *cru* which, strangely, aren't identified as "Beaujolais" on their labels – even though they show off all the region's best traits:

Brouilly

Chénas

Chiroubles

Côte de Brouilly

Fleurie

Juliénas

Morgon

Moulin-á-Vent

Regnie

St-Amour

Bear with me here. I know that Beaujolais is hardly one of the trendiest wine styles around. Its image has been slurried, perhaps, by too many vague recollections of watery, insipid Beaujolais Nouveau, or (worse) light, ordinary red wines from other countries passing themselves off as "Beaujolais". But I want you to try and overcome your prejudice (if you have any) and track down two of the ten *cru* (single village) wines of the region, as opposed to wine labelled Beaujolais-Villages, which is made from grapes sourced from right across the wider district.

A good comparison would be wines from the appellations of Fleurie and Moulin-à-Vent, because although these wines are made from the same red grape variety (Gamay), while they come from neighbouring areas, and while they share characteristics – even the same bright purple-red colour in the glass – they can be noticeably different. Fleurie is usually fleshier, more perfumed (cherries and flowers), while Moulin-à-Vent is more savoury, tannic, and firm. Drink another Beaujolais *cru* from a different village – a Chiroubles, for example – and it'll be different again: lighter, more perfumed. And these differences come from...? Well, the French winemaker would simply say terroir, and shrug his or her shoulders in that life-is-too-mysterious, Gallic way, but you could be more detailed and point to the soil differences. The dirt in Moulin-à-Vent, for example, is richer in minerals than that of Fleurie – hence the stronger, more savoury character in the wine.

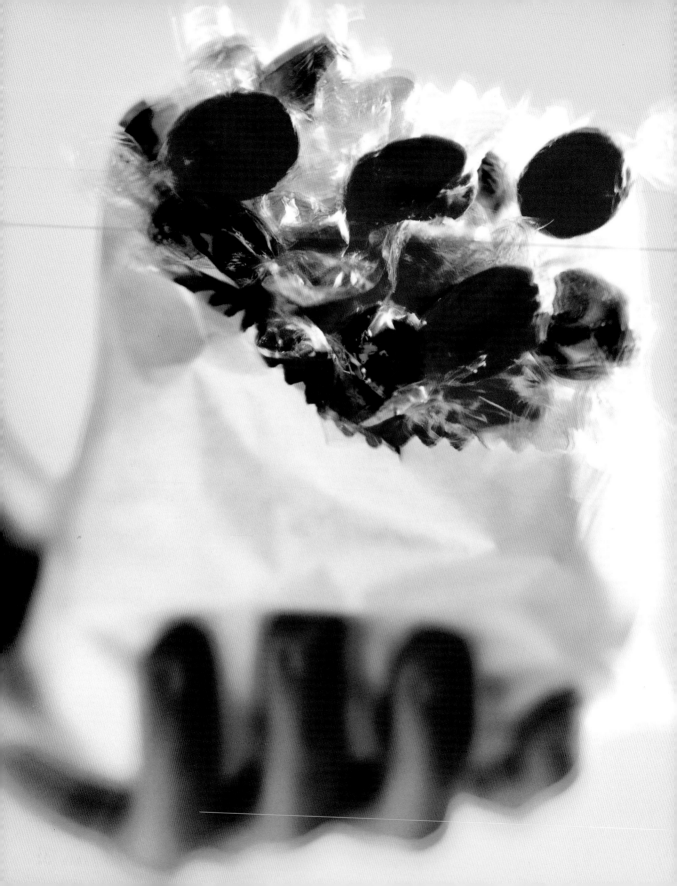

SUGAR, SUGAR
Sweetness in wine

Take a ripe grape, any grape, and hold it between your forefinger and thumb. Now gently squeeze it, letting the clear juice spurt out onto your skin. Hold that position and let the grape juice dry slightly. Feel how tacky it is to the touch? Now lick your fingers (do this as lasciviously as you like, by all means). The first thing you'll taste is sweetness.

The grape is a wonderful fruit for winemakers. It's got all the substances needed to make wine encased inside a skin that's full – as we saw in the first chapter – of flavour. Arguably the most important substance in that little round package is sugar, because without sugar, we wouldn't have alcohol in wine. And let's face it: without alcohol, wine would be a lot less fun than it is.

WHAT SUGAR DOES TO A WINE

As well as being the raw material that yeasts gobble up and turn into alcohol during fermentation, the presence (or absence) of sugar in wine also has a huge impact on the style of the drink in your glass. If there is no sugar at all in the finished wine, it will be fittingly described as "bone-dry", and it will taste mouth-puckeringly lean, like sucking on pebbles. Yet if there's lots of sugar in the finished wine, it can be like a vinous orgasm: soft, honeyed, luscious, and immensely satisfying. These are the extremes, of course, but you get the picture.

The varying sugar levels in your finished wine are a result of how it has been made. If all the sugar in the grapes has fermented into alcohol, then the wine will be dry. If the fermentation is stopped (by chilling and filtering, say) before all the sugar has been converted to alcohol, the wine will be sweet. How sweet depends on when the fermentation was halted. If it's early in the process, there'll be lots of residual sugar; if it's later on, there'll be less, and the wine won't be as sweet. Another way of stopping fermentation is to add alcohol in the form of spirit. This kills the yeasts, leaving some residual sugar and a stronger "fortified" wine (see Wines Your Granny Drinks, page 126). In some countries, adding sugar – often in the form of grape concentrate – to finished, dry wine to make it sweet is permitted, but this usually results in wines that aren't anywhere near as much fun as naturally produced sweet wines.

WHAT ACID DOES TO A WINE

The second most important substance found in your grape is sugar's opposite number: acid. The acids in grapes and wine are fruit acids, such as tartaric and malic acid (also found in apples: imagine biting into a underripe, green Granny Smith), and they give wine its essential zest, life, and juiciness. Just like sugar, the amount of acid in a wine will determine its style – and we're not talking about much here; seven or eight grams per litre is normal. If there's lots of acid in the wine it can taste like sucking on lemons or biting into an apple; not enough acid and the wine will taste flabby, flat, and boring.

As with most things in life, good winemaking is all about balance. If a sweet wine has low acidity, it'll taste sweeter than a wine with exactly the same amount of sugar but higher acidity. The best example of this is that much-maligned wine, German Riesling. It can often contain quite high levels of residual, unfermented sugar, but because it's also quite high in acid, it doesn't always taste immensely sweet. Another example is fortified sweet wine, such as Muscat from Australia. This does taste incredibly rich, but it also has good acidity to keep it alive on your tongue; without acid, it would just taste cloying and really quite repulsive.

CHANGING TASTES

It's a bit of a cliché, and yet it's so true so often: most of us start our alcohol-drinking lives with sweet wines like late-harvest Riesling, then "graduate" to more "sophisticated" dry wines such as Chardonnay before eventually "reverting" to sweet wines like sherry and port when we get older. Responding to sugar, though, is nothing to be ashamed of: it's a distinctly human thing to do. Many of the shrewder New World winemakers know this, and often leave only an almost imperceptible lick of sugar in theoretically dry wines – even "dry" reds like Shiraz and Cabernet Sauvignon – in order to give the impression of softness in the mouth.

FINO

VOUVRAY
DEMI-SEC

RIESLING
AUSLESE

SAUTERNE

PEDRO
XIME

DRINKING IT

The wines we're going to try in this chapter
range from bone-dry (containing no sugar at all)
to teeth-jarringly, lusciously sweet (containing heaps
and heaps of sugar). We'll start with the driest wine,
just as you do at the beginning of a meal, and work
our way up in stages until we indulge in the
sweetest example – as you would at the end of the
same meal. And you'll see: the sugar level in a wine
affects your food choices more strongly than almost
anything else. After all, you'd probably gag at the
thought of drinking bone-dry Chablis with Christmas
cake, or trying a luscious, golden Muscat with
oysters. I would, anyway....

WINE 1: BONE-DRY WHITE

EXAMPLES

Chablis, Muscadet (France)

Frascati, Pinot Grigio, Soave (Italy)

young Hunter Valley Semillon (Australia)

fino sherry, manzanilla sherry (Spain)

Two of the best examples of bone-dry white wine are fino and manzanilla sherries, similar styles that come from south-west Spain. Both of these pale-looking liquids start life as bone-dry, twelve-per-cent alcohol white wines made from very plain-tasting Palomino grapes. They are then only slightly fortified (the alcohol in these wines is about fifteen per cent – not much more than many unfortified Chardonnays), and aged in barrels, protected from oxygen by a layer of the region's characteristic *flor*, or yeast, that contributes a bready flavour and salty tang to the wine.

Drinking these dry sherries on their own (always chilled) can be challenging to modern consumers more used to fruit-rich wines – they are just so savoury, so searingly dry. But drink them with a plate of oysters, for example, and you'll discover that sometimes, coldness, lack of fruit flavour, and (above all) dryness are exactly what you need to complement the salty, slippery texture of these bivalves.

ORDER! ORDER!

There is a very good reason why you serve, and drink, wines from the driest to the sweetest: go the other way, and it just tastes yucky. Try the following experiment at home: drink a bone-dry white, followed by a late-harvest white, followed by a sweet fortified. No problems. Now try it the other way around; I can guarantee the late-harvest and dry wines will taste awful. Like most things to do with wine, this is, of course, just common sense.

ICE-CREAM AND WINE

There are very few food-and-wine combinations that I reckon just don't work, but one of them is ice-cream and sweet wine. This combination doesn't work because the temperature of the ice-cream numbs the tongue and the creaminess clogs the taste-buds. Having said that, the Spanish custom of pouring syrupy Pedro Ximénez sherry over vanilla ice-cream is delicious in the extreme.

WINE 2: MEDIUM-DRY WHITE

EXAMPLES

Verdelho, some unwooded Chardonnay (Australia)

demi-sec **Vouvray** (France)

some New World Sauvignon Blanc, Riesling (the USA, Australia, New Zealand, Chile)

Vouvray is one of those potentially confusing wines, because it comes in many different styles, from bone-dry through medium-dry (i.e. with some residual sugar left after fermentation) to really quite sweet (labelled *moelleux*) and even sparkling. Look for the words *demi-sec* ("half-dry") on the label, however, and you'll find just the white wine I want you to try. The natural apple-fruitiness of the Chenin Blanc grape that is used to make Vouvray is accompanied by a slight honeyed sweetness. For me, that touch of sweetness makes off-dry, fruity whites a great match for aromatic, slightly sweet food such as Thai or Vietnamese fish salads; a touch of sugar in the wine also plays a great counterpoint to the chilli in these and other spicy dishes.

WINE 3: SWEET WHITE

EXAMPLES

Riesling *Spätlese*, Riesling *Auslese* (Germany)

vendange tardive (Alsace, France)

late-harvest Muscat (Australia)

late-harvest Riesling (California, Washington State)

The longer you leave grapes on the vine, the more sugar they will accumulate; thus the later you pick them, the sweeter the wine you can make. A great example of this style of wine is late-harvest Riesling from Germany. Look for a wine with the word *Spätlese* (late-harvest) on the label and you should get aromatic, grapey, perfumed smells, a sweet juiciness in the mouth, and a refreshing, crisp acidity to finish. Because the wine isn't overly sweet, it can be drunk to spectacularly delicious effect with some surprisingly savoury foods. *Spätlese* wines with pâté, game birds like pheasant and pigeon, or Asian-inspired scallops with ginger and lemon grass can be absolutely wonderful.

WINE 4: VERY SWEET, NOBLY ROTTEN WHITE

EXAMPLES

Bonnezeaux, Quarts de Chaume
(Loire, France)

Loupiac, Monbazillac, Sauternes
(Bordeaux, France)

vendange tardive, sélection des grains noble (Alsace, France)

Botrytis Semillon, Riesling
(Australia, New Zealand)

Beerenauslese,
Trockenbeerenauslese (Germany)

Tokáji (Hungary)

noble late-harvest (South Africa)

In some parts of the world, most famously Sauternes in Bordeaux, not only are white grapes left on the vine to ripen after everything else has been picked, but they are also attacked and infected by something called "noble rot" – scientifically speaking, a fungal infection called *Botrytis cinerea*. This airborne fungus has the doubly advantageous effect of both dehydrating the grape (which concentrates the sugar and acidity levels) and contributing a tell-tale and sometimes extraordinary flavour of marmalade or dried apricots. Despite being difficult to make (shrivelled grapes have to be pressed hard to extract the syrupy juice, and fermentation can be unpredictable), the resulting wine, when it's good, is so gloriously rich, complex, and deeply sweet that all the fuss (and cost) is worth it. Botrytis-affected white wines tend to go very well with fruit, cream-based desserts, and blue cheeses.

SOME OTHER STYLES OF SWEET WHITE WINES

♀ *Moscato* (Italy). **About as close to grape juice as it's possible to get. Moscato is bottled halfway through fermentation, with only about five per cent alcohol, gentle sweetness, and natural carbon dioxide fizziness.**
♀ *Eiswein/ice wine* (Germany, Canada). **Occasionally, some grapes manage to hang out as long as the first frosts of winter, when they partially freeze, concentrating the sugar and flavour to an almost unbearable level.**

♀ *Vins doux naturels* (southern France). **Wines like Muscat de Rivesaltes from Roussillon are made by adding neutral spirit to fragrant, sweet, fermenting Muscat wine, then (unlike Australian Muscats) bottling early to retain bright colour and flavour.**
♀ *Passito, Recioto* (Italy). **Ancient way of concentrating sugar and flavour by laying grapes out in the sun on mats to dry: the resulting wines are often very sweet and have noticeable raisiny flavours.**

WINE 5: SUPER-SWEET, FORTIFIED WINE

EXAMPLES

Rutherglen Muscat,
Tokay, Muscadelle (Australia)
Moscatel sherry, Pedro Ximénez
sherry (Spain)

One way of making an extra-sweet wine is to stop fermentation almost as soon as it has begun, leaving most of the sugar unfermented in the wine. And one way of stopping fermentation is by adding alcohol in the form of spirit: the raw alcohol kills the yeasts and leaves you with a strong (eighteen to twenty per cent alcohol by volume), very sweet liquid. In the case of the great, dark-brown super-sweeties like Australia's Muscat and Spain's Pedro Ximénez ("PX" for short), the grapes are also allowed to shrivel to raisins on the vine before being picked, concentrating the flavours and sugars even more. Not surprisingly, such immensely sweet drinks are fabulous with immensely sweet, intense food – like chocolate cake (particularly good with PX), dried fruit, and huge, pongy, feral cheeses – particularly the smelliest blue you can find.

FIREWATER
Wine and alcohol

Let's not beat around the bush here: wine, by definition, contains alcohol. According to the textbooks I've got, the word "wine" means "alcoholic beverage obtained by fermenting grapes" – which kind of nails it, I think. Without alcohol, wine would just be boring grape juice. But there's more to it than that: alcohol plays a crucial role in the warmth, body, persistence of flavour and richness of a wine. It also keeps us coming back for more.

Alcohol, as we all know, is a drug, which is why, in my opinion, wine enjoys such enduring popularity. Oh, we can waffle on (as I've done in the preceding pages) about wine's infinite subtleties and its magical ability to express a particular place on the globe, but if we're honest – if we're *really* honest – most of us love wine because its alcohol makes us feel good when we drink it. Sorry, but it's true and you know it. The last thing you want when you collapse at the end of a hard week with a nice big glass of Chardonnay is to think deeply about malolactic fermentation or elusive hints of grilled hazelnuts. You want to relax and get gently tipsy. Am I right?

A LITTLE HISTORY LESSON

Imagine, if you will, the first humans stumbling across the mood- and mind-altering effects of fermenting fruit. Maybe it was a bunch of grapes hoarded at the back of the cave; in any case, the fruit had begun to bubble as the yeasts on the grape skins began eating away at the sugar-rich juice inside, turning it into alcohol.

Our accidental *vignerons* simply munched on the groggy grapes and got smashed. Sure, they woke up the next day with mankind's first-ever hangover, but their memories of how good the strange-tasting grape

juice made them feel (rather than a discussion of the subtleties of the rank liquid's bouquet) spurred them on to repeat the experience, again and again. And they haven't stopped since.

WHAT ALCOHOL DOES TO A WINE

Of course, alcohol's role in wine is not simply narcotic. As well as being a drug that makes us feel good (or bad, depending on the quantity consumed), alcohol has a huge role to play in the style, structure, and taste of wine. Very basically put, the lower the alcohol, the lighter-bodied the wine; the higher the alcohol, the fuller-bodied the wine.

Also, the level of alcohol in the finished wine is, in most cases, related directly to how much sugar the grapes contained when they were picked; so grapes with thirteen per cent baumé (a measure of sugar content), for example, will make wine that has about thirteen per cent alcohol. For this reason, alcohol and a wine's lightness or heaviness in the mouth are often associated with the climate the grapes were grown in. In the colder parts of Germany, for example, where Riesling grapes often have to struggle to ripen, white wines often have only seven per cent alcohol and taste ethereally light. In sun-drenched California, however, where ripening is much less of a problem, white wines can easily contain twice as much alcohol and taste ten times heavier.

DRINKING TIP: KEEP YOURSELF NICE

As I say, alcohol is a drug – and a poison if imbibed with too much gusto. Which is precisely why I've included some tips for responsible wine drinking – especially if you're at a party or out to dinner with a big group of mates.

♀ Pace yourself. If you can sip rather than swill, you'll slow down the rate of absorption of alcohol into your bloodstream.

♀ Eat, eat, eat. Munching on some food – caviar, kebabs, Pringles®, whatever – also helps slow down the speed with which the drug is taken up by the blood.

♀ Don't mix your drinks. There's a great old saying that goes "beer then wine, you're fine, but wine then beer, you're queer". Apart from having sniggery connotations in this enlightened day and age, it's a pretty good maxim. I'm not sure that the chemistry of mixing the grape with the grain is actually all that bad for you; it's more that if you feel like a palate-cleansing ale to wash down five bottles of Cabernet, it's a sure sign the damage has already been done.

♀ Don't mix your drugs. Smoking when you're drinking wine is a disgusting habit that will make you feel worse the next day. Unless you're smoking a fine cigar and drinking a large glass of the best Shiraz you can afford, in which case I understand completely.

♀ Water, water, everywhere. Same idea as pacing and eating: if you're drinking wine or beer with your meal, try to match every glass of grog with a big glass of fresh, cool water to dilute the effects. We should all drink more water anyway, so now's the time to get into practice.

♀ Drink less, drink better. Such a cliché, but such a good cliché. You're less likely to glug your wine if you paid a week's wages for the privilege, aren't you? Hello?

DRINKING IT

I'm going to kick off this chapter with a nice, average red wine with a common-or-garden amount of alcohol, just to ease you into the idea of tasting the way alcohol affects the body and finish of a wine in your mouth. Then I'm going to pull out all the stops by thrusting three of the strongest wines in the world, from three different countries, at you to show you how lots of alcohol makes drinking red wine quite a different, even formidable, experience. The first three of our heavy hitters are naturally high in alcohol, whereas the last wine is high in alcohol because it's fortified – meaning it has had extra alcohol added to give it a boost.

WINE 1: "NORMAL-STRENGTH" RED WINE

EXAMPLES

reds of twelve per cent alcohol by volume, such as:

cheap Merlot (Bordeaux, Chile, the USA, Australia)

Most of the world's red wine is only twelve per cent (or less) alcohol by volume. Many wine regions can't be bothered to grow riper grapes, or afford the risk that entails; the further into the growing season you get, for example, the greater the chance of rain spoiling your crop. Not only that, but the vines in these regions are often carrying such heavy crops that ripening all the grapes past twelve per cent potential alcohol becomes nigh-on impossible. The heavier the crop, after all, the longer it takes to ripen. But that's fine: the twelve per cent alcohol is what makes a "normal-strength" Merlot easy to drink. It's not too heavy, not too aggressive at the back of the throat, and its medium-bodied friendliness means you can drink a few glasses with dinner.

WINE WORDS

You'll have noticed that I've slipped in a few wine jargon words to keep you on your toes. Words like "lifted" (which means the smells of the wine seem to rocket up your nostrils); "finish" (how the wine feels at the back of the mouth – good or bad?); and "length" (how long the aftertaste lingers down your throat; a long time usually means that the wine's good). And now you know what they mean.

WINE 2: STRONG OLD WORLD RED WINE

EXAMPLES

reds of 13.5+ per cent alcohol by volume, such as:

Châteauneuf-du-Pape (Rhône, France)

Priorato (Cataluna, Spain)

Primitivo di Manduria (Apulia, Italy)

In warmer climates like the southern Rhône Valley in France, where abundant sunshine combines with naturally ripe grapes such as Grenache, planted in naturally yield-reducing stony soils, it has always been possible to make more sugar-rich (and therefore, stronger and more alcoholic) red wines. Find a Châteauneuf-du-Pape with an alcohol content of fourteen per cent (the region is such a reliable ripener that the minimum allowable alcohol content is 12.5 per cent) and see what the difference is.

Don't be put off by the colour: Grenache (the predominant grape variety in this part of the world) can often have a deceptively see-through appearance, making it look lighter than the opaque purple Merlot you've just tried. But smell it and put it in your mouth, and you'll see that just two or three per cent more alcohol gives the wine much more lifted smells, plus more weight, impact, and presence on your tongue and at the back of the throat.

WINE 3: STRONG NEW WORLD WINE

EXAMPLES

reds of fifteen+ per cent alcohol by volume, such as:

late-harvest Zinfandel (California)

late-harvest Grenache,
late-harvest Shiraz (Australia)

In New World wine regions such as California's Napa Valley, which are less encumbered by regulations such as "minimum alcohol content", some winemakers will take advantage of late-summer sunshine and let their red grapes hang and hang, ripening to extreme levels of sugar. If, using turbo-charged yeasts, they convert all this sugar to alcohol during fermentation, the result can be black-as-pitch, heady, powerhouse wines of fifteen+ per cent. These can literally assault the nose and the mouth. Some people argue that the alcohol is too high to make these wines enjoyable; they can taste hot at the back of the throat (literally leaving a burning sensation), and, because alcohol is derived from sugar, lots of it can make these wines taste sweet, even though they have no residual sugar in them. Then again, many people go wild about the very same wines; to them, the stronger they are, the better. Personally, as long as the alcohol is balanced by good flavour and acidity, I don't mind a bit of "oomph".

WINE 4: VINTAGE PORT

EXAMPLES

ports of eighteen per cent alcohol by volume and say five years old, such as:

vintage port (Portugal)

"port styles" (Australia, South Africa, the USA)

Ironically, critics of late-harvest so-called "cult" reds from California (*see page 82*) or Australia are happy to drink vintage port – which seldom has less than eighteen per cent alcohol, and often has twenty. The difference is, I suppose, that you expect port to be strong: it is, after all, a fortified wine. Very ripe local grapes such as Touriga Nacional and Tinta Roriz are picked on the steep, terraced, hillside vineyards of the Douro Valley in northern Portugal, then crushed and fermented. But halfway through fermentation, before all the sugar is fermented away, spirit – almost-pure alcohol – is added to boost the alcohol level and retain some residual sweetness. The result is a dark, purple-coloured wine that, when young, smells and tastes very strongly of that spirit: like prunes and plums macerating in brandy. The high alcohol content also acts as a kind of preservative. The very best port can develop in the bottle for a century or more.

DRINKING TIP: ALCOHOL AND FOOD

As alcohol is so strongly related to the body of a wine, it makes sense to eat lighter foods with lighter alcohol wines, heavier food with stronger wines. Alcohol can also react in really weird ways with chilli: very light wines can be swamped by chilli and other hot spices, while very strong wines can clash horribly with too much heat. The trick is to drink a wine with just enough alcohol to stand up to the chilli, so that the two elements merge to create a pleasing, almost sweet warmth. Unless you're a taste masochist like myself. I do enjoy the odd robust palate-explosion of a scorchingly hot Malaysian fish-head curry accompanied by a seventeen-per-cent alcohol late-harvest Pinot Gris....

GETTING WOOD

What happens when wine is aged in oak barrels

There's much more to ageing wine in wood than building layers of flavour. As wine is pumped into a barrel, as it sits there for eight or twelve months or more, and as it is racked out of the barrel for clarification, it comes into contact with small amounts of oxygen. This softens the wine's texture, harmonizes its flavours, and creates a more mellow, complex drink. The wood itself also contributes some positive structural elements, such as tannin, grip, and astringency. Yet it's those layers of flavour that hit you when you first taste a wood-aged wine.

Flashback time. You're a kid again, running along the beach in one of those eternal, warm, bright summers we enjoyed when we were younger and didn't worry about global warming, mortgages, or the bloody taxman. You've just spent your pocket money on one of those vanilla ice-cream wafer sandwiches. Remember them? A block of golden-yellow ice-cream stuffed tight between two crisp, flaky biscuits, wrapped in silver paper. Remember how they tasted? Rich, creamy, vanilla sweetness of soft ice-cream balanced by the exquisite counterpoint of the more savoury, baked wafer….

Right, hold that thought and flash forward to adulthood. You're in your favourite café, waiting for your first (or maybe second) espresso of the morning, your nostrils twanging to the tantalizing aroma of freshly ground coffee beans: dark, roasted; deeply, sweetly savoury….

Now put all these memories together and you have a pretty good description of the smell (and taste implications) of brand-new, freshly made oak barrels. Despite all the advances in technology, barrels are still made by hand, by bending staves of wood into shape over open flames – hence all those charry, coffee-ground, vanilla flavours. Now think about how those smell-memories make your mouth water. Is it any wonder that winemakers mature their wines in new-oak barrels? They can, after all, confer a sense of grandeur and depth to the wine. Put another way: you pour wine in wood, it tastes better.

HOW WOOD-AGEING DEVELOPED

Traditionally (like, hundreds of years ago), putting wine in barrels was almost solely a logistical issue; the grog had to be stored and shipped in something, and barrels were the common storage and shipping vessels. Most of these barrels would have been old and worn, and there was little or no flavour contribution to the wine from the wood (unless it was mouldy or dirty wood, of course, in which case the contribution was unwelcome). Over the last few decades, however, consumers have been increasingly introduced to/seduced by/hankering for/relishing the distinctive smell of new oak. And as a result, more and more producers now use new-oak barrels in their winemaking. In the case of fuller-bodied wines (Chardonnay in the whites, Shiraz in the reds, say), many winemakers take the process one step further by fermenting their wines in new-oak barrels, resulting in sometimes exaggerated oak characters.

As you might expect, such practices don't come cheap. With good new barrels costing many hundreds of dollars each, wines matured in them can also end up with hefty price tags on the shelf or list. Yet this doesn't mean that cheaper wines are denied the benefit of some oak influence; there are shortcuts to oakiness that many makers of the world's cheaper wines take, such as plunging big tea bags full of oak chips into the wine as it ferments, or lowering big planks of wood into a stainless-steel tank full of wine. But while such techniques can contribute a whack of upfront, vanilla-and-toast flavour, they don't have the same truly complex, mellowing effect gained by ageing the wine inside barrels.

Yet whichever way the oak has been used – the posh way or the budget way – the same rule applies. If the resulting wine isn't balanced, if overt oaky flavour drowns out the fruit, then it's not much fun to drink.

DRINKING TIP: SEDUCTION TIME

As I think I may have mentioned already, the smell and taste of oak can be a very seductive thing. As a result, the obviously oaky wines, with all their sweet vanilla and coconut smells, can often entrance us; they can certainly bewitch the wine-show judges, who tend to favour them over the less oaky, more subtle wines. The trick is not to be seduced: try and taste beyond the oak, and check that there's also enough fruit flavour, persistence of flavour, and palate-satisfaction in the mouth that isn't just wood-derived. If not, the wine will quickly become boring when you try to drink it, and will only develop with age into an older, oaky wine.

DRINKING IT

There are four wines in two sets of pairs I want you to try in this chapter: two unwooded wines (one white, one red) and two wooded wines (one white and one red). The only way to really get a firm picture in your smell-memory of the flavour and taste of wood is to drink, side by side, two versions of the same wine: one that has been aged in an oak barrel, and one that hasn't. As you'll see, such a simple thing as oak influence can have an enormous impact on the style of wine, its complexity, weight in the mouth, richness, etc. – and it also affects the choice of what food you choose to eat with it.

WINE 1: UNWOODED WHITE WINE

WHAT TO LOOK FOR

unwooded Chardonnay from a New World country such as Australia, which will probably have a phrase like "unwooded" or "non-oaked" on the label

We're back in chapter-one territory here, really, because all I expect your unwooded Chardonnay to taste of is – well, Chardonnay. Made from ripe Chardonnay grapes that have been picked, crushed, pressed, and fermented to dryness in cool, stainless steel tanks, the wine will have been bottled young (a couple of months after fermentation) and should be sold young, too – probably within a year or so of its production, so that you can appreciate its fresh flavours of lemon, melon, and apple. You'll perhaps notice that, unlike more famous (and more expensive) traditionally unwooded Chardonnay such as Chablis, from northern Burgundy in France, this New World unwooded Chardonnay is pleasant but fairly one-dimensional – it tastes of ripe white grapes but not much else. As a result, you probably wouldn't want to go out of your way to cook anything too posh to eat with it: some fish and chips, perhaps, or simple antipasti.

WINE 2: OAK-MATURED WHITE WINE

WHAT TO LOOK FOR

you guessed it: wooded Chardonnay, with phrases such as "aged in oak", "barrel-fermented" on the back label – preferably from the same country, region, or, if you can find it, the same vineyard or winemaker

Even the colour should tell you that this wine is going to be different. Unlike the unwooded Chardonnay, which was really quite pale, this will probably be more of a golden yellow. Why? Because after the ripe Chardonnay grapes have been crushed, pressed, and fermented (possibly even in the barrel), the wine comes into gentle contact with oxygen in oak, and, just like any fruit exposed to oxygen, it goes a slightly darker colour. The smells and flavours are quite different, too, thanks to the wine having been in contact with the wood. As well as the apple and lemon, there's another layer of vanilla and toast, following through in the mouth to give the wine a rounder, richer, more complex taste. All of which makes me think of posher food: garlicky, herby roast chicken's very good, as is barbecued lobster (if you can afford it), or other grilled seafood and creamy sauces. Certainly, fuller-flavoured, rich foods do well with barrel-aged Chardonnay.

WHEN YOU'RE YOUNG, SIZE *DOES* MATTER

The younger and smaller the oak barrels being used, the more obvious the oak influence will be. The more the barrel is used, and the larger it is, the less the oaky flavour will be imparted to the wine. Barriques (225-litre capacity) are probably the most commonly encountered barrels in wineries around the world (you'll see the phrase "barrique-aged" or something similar on wines from Bordeaux to Santa Barbara), while many producers, particularly in Australia, use slightly larger barrels called hogsheads (300 litres).

WINE 3: UNWOODED RED WINE

EXAMPLES

reds of twelve months old or less, such as:

Rioja *joven* (Spain)
Beaujolais (France)
Dolcetto (Italy)

I love Rioja. It's arguably Spain's most famous red wine and, as well as the best examples being damn fine drinks, it's incredibly useful for demonstrating the flavour of wood in wine to people. Take, for example, a young Rioja with the word *joven* ("young") on the label. According to Spanish law, this wine has to be sold the year after its vintage and is almost never matured in oak, so what you get is a bright, purple-red wine, quite light in body, quite soft, and with the typical red fruit and almost sweet-cherry flavour of the main Rioja red grapes, Tempranillo and Garnacha. Perfect for drinking in copious quantity as one ambles from one tapas bar to the next on a warm, late summer's evening in Madrid (as you do)....

BUT WHICH OAK TO USE?

Just as different growing conditions, soils, and grape varieties produce wines with different characters, so there can be quite strong differences between types of oak, depending on where it's from, and how it's made, and who made it, and how heavily charred it was, and how long it was seasoned before it was made into barrels. In fact, you could spend your life delving into the murky world of oak appreciation. Some winemakers insist that fine-grained oak from the Tronçais forest in France, for example, has the perfect qualities of finesse and tight tannins for ageing Cabernet Sauvignon. While looser-grained white oak from Kentucky, USA, with its obvious coconut flavour and sweetness, is better for Shiraz. Unless it's cooler-climate Shiraz, of course, in which case a blend of different oaks made by a cooper (barrel-maker) in Burgundy is the stuff. There's a whole new book in this, I reckon.

WINE 4: OAK-MATURED RED WINE

EXAMPLES

the best example of an obviously wood-influenced wine, such as:

Rioja *reserva*, Rioja *gran reserva* (Spain)

riserva (Italy)

"reserve" (the USA, Australia, New Zealand, South Africa)

Look (and smell, and taste) what happens to those Tempranillo and Garnacha grapes when they're fermented and then aged in oak barrels for a year or more (again, by law *reserva* wines have to spend at least one year in barrel, *gran reserva* wines two years, while some very traditional Rioja producers keep their top wines in barrel for even longer). The wine is a different colour for a start: the contact with air has turned it from a bright purple into a paler, redder, even slightly browning-at-the-edges colour. The smells and flavours are much more savoury; as well as the red fruit, there's leather and vanilla, spice, and coffee. And the wine is drier, more astringent, more tannic-grippy, more complex – the kind of majestic red wine, I would have thought, you'd want to mull over while relaxing with a large platter of charcoal-grilled lamb and red peppers, or chorizo sausages and crusty bread.

FIDDLING AROUND

The winemakers craft: blending grape varieties, barrels, and vintages

Almost every single wine you drink is a blend in one form or another. The most obvious examples of this are traditional French red wines such as Côtes du Rhône, which is nearly always a blend of Grenache, Syrah, Mourvèdre, and a host of other red grape varieties; or sparkling wines such as Champagne, which is more often than not a blend of Pinot Noir and Chardonnay grapes, and is usually a blend of wines from different vintages.

But even if the label tells you that the wine is made from one grape variety, picked from one vineyard, and made at one winery, the finished product will still probably be a blend: a blend of the dozens of different barrels the wine was aged in, or a blend of half the vineyard's fruit, which was picked a week earlier than the other half of the fruit.

WHAT BLENDING DOES TO A WINE

So why is blending such a common practice in the winery? Well, to answer this question, it's worth remembering that wine is a *food* – albeit a liquid, alcoholic food. And as with all food, while one top-quality ingredient can taste delicious, a whole meal made up of many different ingredients is often a much more pleasurable experience. A single, perfectly ripe, organic, vine-ripened tomato, for example, is a wondrous thing; but combine that tomato with some pungent basil, some sweet, fresh buffalo mozzarella, a drizzle of green olive oil, and perhaps a few grinds of black pepper, and you have a completely satisfying, complex, intense dish.

The fundamental reason for blending is to make better wine. While Cabernet Sauvignon and Merlot on their own can each make good red wine in Bordeaux (and many other placesr), if you put them together, they make something that is more than the sum of its parts, the fleshiness of

the Merlot combining wonderfully with the sturdy dryness of the Cabernet. In many cases, historically, blending arose from necessity, with some grapes being used to bolster others. So, while the later-ripening Cabernet Sauvignon is the grape most people readily associate with Bordeaux (the region and the wine), in fact, more vines of the earlier ripening (therefore more reliable) Merlot are planted there.

HOW BLENDING KEEPS WINE NICE

At the cheaper end of the spectrum, there are other good reasons for blending, the major one being to ensure the quantity and consistency of the product. The vast-production, branded wines from Australia and the USA, for instance, which account for millions of cases each, are often blends of grapes from dozens of different vineyards, sometimes located thousands of miles apart. If the vintage is warm and strong, then the blends will contain higher proportions of lighter, higher-acid wines from cooler regions to balance the riper, rounder flavours from the warm vineyards. If the vintage is cooler and more difficult, then the blend will contain more of the riper-tasting wine from the warmer regions. In both cases, however, the end result should taste about the same.

Yet blending isn't easy, let me tell you. Many's the time I've made a complete idiot of myself in front of winemakers I respect, simply by trying to make my own blend out of various component samples of wine from their barrels; no matter how clever I reckon I'm being at the time, their blend always tastes better. Blending is hard because adding A to B doesn't just make something that tastes like A plus B; it creates a new wine that tastes like C. Adding a sweet wine to an acidic wine, for example, doesn't just create a sweeter wine; it also creates a wine with less obvious acidity. Decisions about how much of this to mix in with that, therefore, are where the skill (dare we say "art"?) of the winemaker comes to the fore.

IN PRAISE OF THE INDIVIDUAL

It all depends on how I'm feeling. Sometimes I love the complexity, the harmony, and layers of flavour to be gleaned from a good bottle of wine that has been blended from two or three grape varieties. It's like listening to a great band at the height of its creative powers on a good night. But sometimes, I like to drink a single-varietal wine from a single small vineyard and appreciate its purity. Like listening to a single, mournful saxophone, or violin, or voice, each note it produces is as clear as a bell.

DRINKING IT

As I say, almost every wine you drink is a blend in one form or another, so finding blends to try shouldn't be too hard. The following are just four examples; you'll also encounter many other blended wines in the other chapters of this book. Another good way of learning about blends is to find a wine whose label lists the component grape varieties (Sémillon and Chardonnay, for example), then find a varietal Sémillon and varietal Chardonnay from the same producer or region. Sample the three at the same time to see how the flavours and tastes of the individual grapes affect each other when they're blended.

WINE 1: NON-VINTAGE SPARKLING WINE

EXAMPLES

non-vintage Champagne (France)

sparkling Pinot Noir/Chardonnay (Australia, New Zealand, the USA)

cava (Cataluna, Spain)

This is the idea: every time you open a bottle of non-vintage sparkling wine, whether it be an expensive bottle of absolutely fabulous Champagne or a cheap-as-chips, black-frosted bottle of cava, the wine inside the bottle should taste just the same as the wine inside any of the bottles that bears the same label, regardless of the year it was made. To achieve this, the winemaker will take a few different, complementary grape varieties – in the case of cava, these are traditionally the pretty boring-tasting Macabeo, the fuller, gutsier Xarel-lo and the sometimes quite fine and citric Parellada – and each year blend them together to make a "house" style of wine. To ensure even more consistency, the final bottled wine will often include component wines from a few different years, because by judiciously blending riper-tasting, better wines from better vintages with more acidic, crisper-tasting wines from lesser vintages, the house style can be maintained. This is a good thing, as most of the occasions in which you'd be tempted to open some fizz don't call for studied contemplation of each and every bottle, do they?

WINE 2: BLENDED WHITE WINE

EXAMPLES

Bordeaux Blanc (France)

Semillon/Sauvignon Blanc (Australia)

Increasingly, as wineries modernize their operations and look to global, wine-savvy markets, the tradition of blending white grapes is disappearing from Bordeaux. If you picked up a white Bordeaux a couple of decades ago, it would have been a very dry, savoury blend of Sémillon, Sauvignon Blanc, and Muscadelle, aged in oak barrels. These days it is just as likely to be straight Sémillon or perhaps a blend with Sauvignon Blanc, and it'll probably be fruitier-tasting and fresher, with the rich, lemony characteristics of Sémillon boosted by the grassier, crisper qualities of the Sauvignon, and the tangy vanilla oak playing a less savoury, more subtle role. This is a good example of how some so-called traditional blends can evolve and even disappear, but I'm not sure it's a development I'm entirely happy with. The newer styles of white Bordeaux aren't necessarily as good with food (grilled fish, simple sauces, salads) as the old blends were.

THINKING OUTSIDE THE BOX

Some grape varieties have shown over the centuries that they go very well together, complementing each other's characters and creating distinctive wines. Good examples include the blending of a little of the aromatic white grape Viognier with the purple spiciness of Syrah in the red wines of the northern Rhône Valley; and the full fruitiness and breadth of flavour of Pinot Noir blended with the finesse and length of flavour of Chardonnay in Champagne and other top-quality sparkling wines. As the wine world has become more adventurous over the last few decades, however, we are also seeing an increasing number of new, interesting, and exciting blends: the "Burgundian" grape (Chardonnay) blended with the "Rhône" grape (Roussanne), for example, and "Italian" grapes like Sangiovese being blended with "international" grapes such as Cabernet and Merlot. I'd like to see more of this kind of experimentation, because it pushes the boundaries of flavour and creates more exciting wines for the consumer.

WINE 3 & WINE 4: BLENDED RED WINE

EXAMPLES

Chianti (Italy)

Valpolicella (Italy)

Bordeaux (France)

Côtes du Rhône (France)

Rioja (Spain)

Meritage (the USA)

Cabernet Sauvignon/Shiraz
(Australia)

A very good example of traditional, distinctly regional (i.e. only produced in one part of the world) blended red wine is Valpolicella, from vineyards located just to the north of Verona, in the Veneto region of north-east Italy. A blend of three local red grapes (Corvina, Molinara, and Rondinella) that are not widely planted at all outside this one region, Valpolicella in its basic form is notable for its relatively light colour, its light, cherry-and-almond-like aroma, and light-to-medium-bodied, grippy, astringent taste. It's when you drink the richer forms of Valpolicella made from grapes that have been partially dried out – the sweet Recioto wines; the dark, dry, strong, sometimes bitter Amarone wines – that you taste why these particular grapes do so well when made into wine together in this part of the world. You also taste wine that simply could not be mistaken for anything else.

To find a stark contrast to this highly localized, ancient approach to winemaking, open a bottle of commercial Australian branded red wine. It may well tell you on the label that the wine is a blend of two or more "international" grape varieties (which means they are grown in wine regions all over the world), probably the ubiquitous Cabernet Sauvignon and Shiraz; the latter's warmth and richness of flavour is used to complement the former's famously stern astringency. What it probably won't tell you in such clear terms is that the wine is a blend of grapes grown in many different vineyards, in different regions, even in different states. In order to consistently supply millions of cases of affordable, reliable grog, this inter-regional blending is quite commonplace with popular branded wines, a process that perhaps sacrifices individuality and distinct character in favour of a more formulaic user-friendliness. Interestingly, though, some of Australia's most expensive, sought-after, and thoroughly characterful wines are also blends of the best fruit from more than one region – which is a convincing argument that great wines don't necessarily have to taste of a single vineyard.

WINE LAWS

Most of the traditional wine-growing regions of the world have laws about which grape varieties you can and can't grow and use if you want to put the regional name on your label. So when you pick up a bottle of red Bordeaux, for example, you know that it can contain only the varieties Cabernet Sauvignon, Merlot, Cabernet Franc, Malbec, and Petit Verdot (and it probably only contains the first two). It will definitely not contain Syrah. Most of the newer wine-growing districts are much more relaxed about this kind of thing, and tend to go by the "if it's on the label, it must be true" principle – so wine-growers can plant and cultivate whatever varieties they like, but if the label says the wine is a blend of Cabernet and Merlot, then that's what must be inside the bottle. Having said that, however, many wine countries do have a small amount of leeway. In Australia, for example, if your label says Shiraz, only eighty-five per cent of the wine has to be Shiraz; it is legally allowed to contain up to fifteen per cent of anything else, which gives the winemaker significant options for blending.

DRINKING TIP: MATCHING FOOD AND WINE

One way to think about matching food and wine is to treat the wine as another ingredient of the dish you're cooking or ordering. So just as you'd naturally squeeze a wedge of lemon or lime over a grilled piece of white, flaky fish, you'd probably also naturally enjoy a zingy, acidic, young and unwooded white wine to go with it. And just as you might accompany a piece of roast or barbecued meat with a rich, reduced, deeply savoury gravy or sauce, then you might also want to try a rich, savoury, dense, full-bodied red wine along with it.

OLD VERSUS NEW

What's the difference between New World wines and Old World wines?

A particularly pedantic mate of mine is going to be livid when he reads this chapter, because he can't stand the phrases "New World" and "Old World" being applied to wine. Even though the distinction is made and the two phrases are used all the time whenever people talk about the global wine trade (I've used them myself all the way through this book), my mate has made it his personal mission to eradicate their usage from the English language.

He argues that describing countries such as the USA and South Africa as "new", when both have histories of wine production stretching back over 300 or 400 years, is just as ludicrous and demeaning as applying the word "old" to a winemaker in France even if he or she has only been making wine for a couple of weeks. He also reckons it's unacceptably Anglo-centric.

I can see his point. But even he is willing to admit that there is a difference between "traditional" winemaking as practised for centuries in Europe – techniques learned and passed down from generation to generation; emphasis on structure and savour of the wine; use of grape varieties restricted by law, etc. – and "modern" winemaking associated with countries such as Australia, New Zealand, the USA, and South Africa: techniques learned at wine school; emphasis on fruit flavour and sweetness; unrestricted use of grape varieties, etc.

So perhaps a better way to distinguish between traditional and modern is to use the phrases "old-fashioned" and "new-fashioned". After all, there are some staunchly traditional fifth-generation winemakers in Australia, just as there are progressive, innovative first-generation winemakers in Europe. There are also winemakers in both camps who use both tradional and modern techniques to good – or not so good – effect. Confused? Let me explain.

WHEN WORLDS COLLIDE

My mate's also got another good point, however, in that it's becoming harder and harder to say with any confidence that old-fashioned wines come from the Old World and new-fashioned wines come from the New World. If anything, the most interesting New World winemakers (Australian, American, New Zealand, etc.) are moving more and more toward old-fashioned techniques in the vineyard and winery, while the most interesting Old World winemakers (French, Spanish, Italian, etc.) are moving further and further toward new-fashioned techniques in their vineyards and wineries. And while you'd think that the result would be everybody's wines tasting the same, in fact, the opposite is true.

Sure, at the cheaper end (and occasionally the more expensive end) it's sometimes hard to tell whether the Chardonnay in your glass is from France, Chile, or South Africa. Yet for every bland, internationalized wine, there is a truly exciting alternative: a South Australian Shiraz, for example, that has been made using ancient techniques developed in Burgundy and has an extra level of texture and structure; or a Spanish Tempranillo made using Australian technology that has an extra layer of pure, varietal fruit flavour.

GRAPES THAT GET AROUND

Another aspect of all this toing and froing from the old to the new is the migration of grape varieties. Vines have travelled all over the world for millennia, of course, and some, such as Syrah/Shiraz, have histories in the New World that are almost as long and rich as their histories in the Old World. But more recent developments have come about as a direct result of people trying to innovate. A good example is the red grape called Petit Verdot. In its traditional region of Bordeaux, its late-ripening tendency and high acidity levels mean that it only ever takes a minor role in a blend alongside Merlot and Cabernet Sauvignon. Yet in the warmer regions of Australia, where it has only recently been planted widely, it ripens much more reliably, has softer acidity, and is beginning to produce some exciting wines that traditional winemakers in Bordeaux probably wouldn't even recognize.

This is one of the things I love most about being involved in the wine game. In these days of blurred boundaries between the traditional and the modern, you often get the opportunity to drink truly new wines with flavours nobody has ever experienced before.

DRINKING IT

With this bunch, I want to show you a traditional, old-fashioned wine, a typically new-fashioned wine, and then a wine that somehow combines both the old and the new. The reds are easy and recognizable – they're all made from Pinot Noir. Yet you may not be so familiar with a couple of the whites, which highlights the fact that there are thousands of different grape varieties planted across the world, and most of us only ever drink about a dozen of them (Chardonnay, Cabernet Sauvignon, Merlot, etc.). We owe it to our palates and pleasure-buds to be more adventurous.

WINE 1: OLD-FASHIONED WHITE WINE

EXAMPLES

arguably the best country for fiercely traditional (euphemism for "dry as buggery, fruitless, and dilute") white wine is Italy; look for wines such as:

Gavi, Greco di Tufo, Soave, Verdicchio (Italy)

How can we put this nicely? Traditionally, Italian dry white wine hasn't enjoyed the most glowing reputation, thanks to ordinary grape varieties such as boring old Trebbiano, high-cropping vineyards producing dilute flavours, and less-than-hygienic winemaking. But despite this, open a bottle of young, traditional Soave, say, from the Veneto region of Italy, and you'll discover that its very dry, almost flavourless tang is actually the perfect thing to drink with seafood and antipasto. The problem with this exercise, of course, is that the Soave may have been made by a "new-fashioned" winemaker using lower-yield fruit and clean, cool, stainless steel fermentation – in which case it'll be fruitier, richer, and much more fun. Which is fine, but it kind of ruins the punch-line.

LET THE VINE GO THIRSTY

The grapevine, according to some growers, is like a weed: give it fertile soil and lots of water and it will flourish. The problem is, you don't want your vine to flourish – unless you're into producing huge quantities of grapes for very cheap wine. Instead, the best vineyards in both the old- and the new-fashioned wine regions tend to be planted on hungrier soil, and have little or no supplementary irrigation. In most European countries, irrigation is forbidden. On labels of wines from "New World" countries, look for words like "dry-grown" for an indication that the wine's producer is aiming for quality.

WINE 2 & WINE 3: NEW-FASHIONED WHITE WINE

EXAMPLES

Chardonnay (Tuscany, Italy)
Catarratto (Sicily, Italy)
Vermentino (Sardinia, Italy)

Chardonnay is not new to Italy. It has been grown there – as has that other "international" variety, Merlot – for centuries. But in recent times, more and more Italian growers have planted it and winemakers have made it to export to thirsty restaurant-goers in London and New York. Taste a Tuscan Chardonnay, however, and while it starts off tasting familiar – the peachy fruit, the creamy oak – it almost always finishes off tasting irretrievably Tuscan, with dry, mineral flavours and a twist of almond right on the back of the palate.

On the other hand, I've had new-wave Vermentino from Sardinia (both the grape variety and the island were thought of as extremely traditional until recently) that has been made in such a New World way (cool, stainless steel fermentation, bottled early, etc.) that it could have been a lightly aromatic Sauvignon Blanc from Australia, with lifted, perfumed, lemony fruit flavours and crisp, refreshing, clean acidity. Interestingly, though, in both cases, you'll find that neither the use of a "modern" grape variety or "modern" winemaking has eradicated either of these Italian white wines' ability to partner traditional Italian white-wine-friendly foods: deep-fried, floured little fish; green olives; crusty bread; herby frittata....

WINE 4: OLD-FASHIONED RED WINE

WHAT TO LOOK FOR

there are still a number of countries churning out old-fashioned red wine, but for the sake of this try:

red burgundy (France)

The traditional Burgundian wine cellar is everything you imagine when you picture "The Winemaker" in your mind's eye: old bloke in overalls pottering among the barrels in his dusty, candlelit underground cavern, slowly drawing red wine from the cask and squirting it into your glass to taste. The main driving force behind this winery and winemaker is the desire to make a wine that speaks of where it's from and tastes really good with roast game birds – you know the kind of thing: guinea fowl marinated in juniper berries and bay leaves, slowly spit-roasted.... As a result, there is not the same level of ripe fruit flavour you'd expect from, say, an Australian Pinot Noir, but instead there is a savouriness, a dryness, an underlying earthiness that makes the wine good to drink on its own, but much more enjoyable with food.

DRINKING TIP: OLD VINES, OLD FOOD

The rediscovery of long-forgotten indigenous grape varieties has a strong parallel in the food world, with heritage vegetables, livestock, and cheeses being documented and protected and preserved by organizations such as the Slow Food movement. Not surprisingly, old-fashioned food tends to taste best with old-fashioned wine, probably from the same region. Try slow-cooked, savoury roasts, for instance, with tannic, barrel-aged red wines, or rich, creamy fish dishes with crisp, minerally, Chablis-like Chardonnay.

LONG-LOST FRIENDS

One of the most exciting things that's happened in the wine world over the last twenty or so years has been the rediscovery and proud redeployment of many of the world's indigenous, overlooked, discarded, and spurned grape varieties. No sooner had the flying winemakers gone fluttering all over the face of the globe, imposing the Chardonnay and Cabernet Empire on unsuspecting supermarket consumers everywhere ("McDonaldizing" wine, if you like) than a band of vinous anti-globalization protesters reacted by rooting around in their backyards to see how they could assert their identity. The Chileans, for example, discovered that much of what they thought was Merlot was, in fact, Carmenère, a grape variety that had all but been wiped out in its traditional home of Bordeaux. The Italians have had a field-day sticking up for the rights of Vermentino, Aglianico, Corvina, and Greco di Tufo, while the Spanish have a wonderful indigenous, modern grape in the form of Albariño, from Rías Baixas on the north-west coast. All of which gives you, the wine drinker, a wider choice of flavours and experiences to choose from.

DRINKING TIP: NEW WINES, NEW FOOD

On the other hand, it will probably come as no surprise when I say that new-fashioned wines, with their sweet, ripe fruit, their juicy acidity, and softer tannins, tend to go better with what we might consider to be "new-fashioned food". Try bright, unwooded, aromatic white wine with fresh, aromatic, Asian-inspired salads, for example, or sweet-sauced grilled meats with sweetly oaky, alcoholic, warm-climate red wine, or even sparkling red.

AGE SHALL NOT WEARY THEM

The conventional wisdom in the wine world is that the older a vine gets, the more concentrated the grapes and the better the wine – and that good wine cannot be made until the vineyard is ten or twelve years old, at least. This, some people argue, is where the Old World (sorry), has it all over the New: old, mature, well-established vineyards producing wine with more focus and length of flavour. And it's true that, while some of the New World (sorry, sorry) is blessed with very old vines, most of the vineyards are relatively young – one explanation, perhaps, for the relative simplicity of some Australian and California wines, for example. As a result, the phrases *vieilles vignes* or "old vines" are appearing more and more on wine labels as claims to quality; for more on this, see the last chapter in this book, "Going Back To Your Roots", page 134.

WINE 5 & WINE 6: NEW-FASHIONED RED WINE

EXAMPLES

to contrast the old-fashioned
red burgundy, try:

Pinot Noir (New Zealand; Oregon,
the USA)

"new-wave" red burgundy
(France)

The 1980s and '90s saw an explosion of mostly small, committed, quality-focussed producers across the New World, eking out small quantities of mostly expensive red wines made from Pinot Noir, many of which were shamelessly modelled on what are perceived to be "Burgundian" winemaking techniques: low-yielding vines planted close together to limit yield even further, concentrating flavours; hand-plunged, slow, open fermentations; minimal filtration – all that malarkey. The results can be wonderful, stewed-cherry/forest-floor/velvet-textured Pinots that have elements of the New World (ripe fruit) but also some of the savoury elements and complexity of the Old.

Just as the Americans (and Aussies, and Kiwis, and South Africans) began really digging the Pinot/Burgundy groove in the '80s and '90s, copying all those Old World techniques and making burgundy look-alike wines, along came the next generation of young Burgundian winemakers. These guys and gals had travelled through the Napa Valley (the USA), done a vintage in the Barossa (Australia), knew about the impact a good review in America could have on sales, and they began applying more new-fashioned techniques, such as picking the fruit riper, cold-soaking the crushed red grapes before fermentation to extract more bold fruit flavour and colour, maturing (even fermenting) the wine in brand-new, heavily toasted, charred oak barrels, etc., etc. And the result? Well, blow me down if these new-wave red burgundies don't often taste disarmingly like top-notch Pinot Noir from Oregon (the USA) or Martinborough (New Zealand).

TALL, DARK, & HANDSOME
Full-bodied wines

There can be a lot of macho bravado involved in the drinking of Big Red Wines. You know what I'm talking about: you're at a restaurant that specializes in steak, say, and the place is full of blokes pouring big glasses of black-as-pitch Cabernet or Zinfandel; tucking into bloodied rib-eyes; slathering on the horseradish, hot mustard, and chilli sauce; opening more bottles; and generally behaving like Vikings. The bigger the better, too, as far as our heroic drinkers are concerned; they're only happy when chewing on fifteen-per-cent alcohol, dense, syrupy fluid that would scare the living daylights out of a light, fresh, water-white Riesling.

The thing is, the more the consumers and critics scream for bigger and bolder wines, the more winemakers seem happy to oblige. There's a winemaker I know who makes huge red wines – wines that resemble rugby forwards or sumo wrestlers – and every year he tries to outdo his efforts from the previous vintage by picking his grapes riper, extracting more and more tannin and colour and flavour from those grapes by mashing them up more vigorously in the fermentation vat, letting the wine macerate with the grape skins for longer and longer, and ageing the wine in brand-new, heavy-char oak barrels. Oh, and he likes listening to thumping, hard-core rock music, too.

WHY BALANCED IS BETTER

Now I confess that I love indulging in a bit of Viking role-play myself on occasion, and have a soft spot for Big Red Wines so massive and full-bodied that you can stand a spoon in them. Sometimes I like to eat full-flavoured, gutsy food and listen to thumping, hard-core rock music, too.

Yet I also like a bit of balance. In the case of most red wines, there are four elements combining in your mouth: alcohol, tannin (the astringent grippiness extracted from the grape skins and oak during fermentation and maturation), acidity, and flavour. What makes the wine "Big" is a high level of alcohol, lots of tannin, mostly (but not necessarily) soft acidity, and heaps

of flavour (also extracted from the grape skins by fermentation). If the wine is hugely tannic and grips your tongue and gums with the force of a wharf labourer before finally, reluctantly letting go and clomping down your throat, but doesn't have enough fruit or richness to balance the dryness, then it won't be too pleasant. Likewise, if the wine's alcohol completely dominates, it'll end up tasting hot and clunky.

If the acid is too soft, the wine will be cloying; too high and it'll highlight the tannin even more. And if there's not enough flavour – either primary fruit flavour extracted from the grapes or complex secondary flavours that come from fermentation, maturation, and bottle-age – then the wine will end up tasting hollow and tough.

HOW TO MAKE A GOOD BIG WINE

The trick is to get all these elements working in harmony. So the winemaker needs to use grape varieties that are high in flavour, sugar, and tannin, varieties like those I've chosen as examples on the next few pages. The winemaker then needs to pick the grapes ripe (but not too ripe), with enough sugar to create lots of alcohol but before the acidity levels have dropped off too far. Then, in the winery, those grapes need to be crushed, put into fermentation vats, and – without putting too fine a point on it – have the living bejesus thrashed out of the skins to extract as much of the flavour and tannin as is required.

Traditionally, this extraction was achieved by people jumping into the vat and stomping up and down on the crushed grapes, or by repeatedly plunging the skins down through the fermenting juice, or pumping the wine frequently over the skins. Fermenting at warm temperatures and then leaving the wine in contact with the skins for a while after fermentation also aids the process.

More recently, techniques such as fermenting the crushed grapes in huge, revolving tanks has shortened the process without sacrificing any of the extraction. Also, finishing fermentation in new-oak barrels is an increasingly popular technique for adding another layer of flavour, with the toasty, charry, savoury flavours of the barrel's insides being leached into the wine (*see* "Getting Wood", page 48).

DRINKING IT

Not all full-bodied wines are red, of course, despite what the Big-Wine-lovers tell you. To prove it, we'll start this chapter's batch of wines with a white. Then it's straight back into red territory, with some of the biggest, boldest wines around, both from traditional wine regions, made using traditional techniques, and from new wine regions using much more modern techniques. To soak up the alcohol and give your mouth some relief from all the tannin, extract, and flavour, get in some Big-Wine-friendly food before you open the bottles. Steak's good, but a good, crumbly, hard cheese is also a delicious accompaniment.

WINE 1: FULL-BODIED WHITE WINE

WHAT TO LOOK FOR

oak-aged whites of fourteen+ per cent alcohol by volume – the Viognier grape variety is a good bet; try:

Condrieu (Rhône, France)

Viognier (California, South Australia)

The fundamental difference between Big Whites and Big Reds, of course, is that whites don't usually contain much tannin; they are made by fermenting the crushed and pressed juice only, perhaps with some grape-skin contact to build texture and flavour in the wine before fermentation. With whites, bigness comes more from alcohol and flavour, and, in the case of fat-textured, aromatic varieties like Viognier, partially from a higher level of glycerol, produced during fermentation. High alcohol, in particular, as we've seen, gives more body and palate-impact to a wine, as do techniques such as barrel-fermentation, stirring of the lees, and malolactic fermentation.

So Viognier (and Chardonnay) grown in a warm climate, picked ripe, barrel-fermented, and frequently stirred before bottling, can often taste as full-bodied as, say, a soft-tannin red wine such as Pinot Noir. Indeed, block your nose (so you can't distinguish the aromas and flavours), taste a full-bodied Chardonnay next to a medium-bodied Pinot, and you'll probably not be able to tell them apart.

DRINKING TIP: EQUIP YOURSELF

Opening a brace of Big Wines, or even just one bottle, is the best excuse to dust off the hardcore, big-fishbowl glassware. The more air and slooshing you can give to full-bodied, full-flavoured wines in your glass, whether they're white or red, the more they tend to open out and give you more pleasure. The idea is that contact with oxygen helps to soften a wine's soft edges, loosen up the flavours, and reveal some of the fruit hiding in among all that tannin and alcohol – not a very technical description, I know, but one that certainly conveys what I see happening when I sloosh Big Wines around.

DRINKING TIP: BIG WINES AND BIG FOOD

This is going to seem so blatantly obvious that you'll probably want to give me a slap, but Big Wines need Big Food to accompany them. Yes, I know: it's common sense. But so much of wine is, really. If you're drinking something that's warm, ripe, full of grippy tannin, and fills every crevice of your mouth with flavour and extract and oomph, then dainty little asparagus *vol-au-vents* probably aren't going to be able to live up to the task: they will literally be swamped by the weight of the wine. I know it's shamelessly carnivorous of me to say so, but you really can't do better than a nice hunk of roasted or barbecued red meat when you're drinking Big Reds (Big Whites need lobster or similarly rich seafood, I reckon). It's the tannins, you see: they combine so well with the fat and protein in the flesh, literally breaking it down in your mouth and creating a wonderfully satisfying sensation on the tongue. Be careful, though, with chilli – too much spicy heat can clash with obvious tannins, especially if they're the harsher tannins from oak barrels rather than from grape tannins.

WINE 2: OLD-FASHIONED BIG RED

WHAT TO LOOK FOR

traditional wine regions renowned for their tannic, tough, and sturdy reds, such as:

Barolo, Barbaresco – made from Nebbiolo (Piedmont, Italy)

Basilicata – made from Aglianico (southern Italy)

Châteauneuf-du-Pape (Rhône, France)

Grenache-based wines (Rhône, France)

Bandol – made from Mourvèdre (Provence, France)

I love Nebbiolo. Even the best traditional examples of the grape, from Barolo or Barbaresco in Piedmont, can be disarmingly pale; the grape simply doesn't often have as much colour in its skins as Cabernet Sauvignon or Shiraz. As a result, Nebbiolo can often look like rusty water – quite pale and browning at the edges – and you expect it to taste correspondingly pale and light. But smell the wine, and, if it's good, it can assault your nostrils with an extraordinarily complex, powerful aroma of freshly dug earth, macerated plums, spice, and fading flowers. Then put it in your mouth and the first thing that hits you is the tannin: a brusque, savoury dryness that holds on to your tongue and crawls across it and down your throat. Nebbiolo might not be full in fruit-flavour terms, and it's certainly not strong in oak flavours (it is traditionally aged in large old barrels that contribute little oakiness), but it is positively huge in terms of structure.

WINE 3: NEW-FASHIONED BIG RED

WHAT TO LOOK FOR

a tannic red variety that produces more robust examples than in its home region of Bordeaux; such as:

Cabernet Sauvignon (California, South Africa, South Australia)

Put a glass of good, young California Cabernet Sauvignon next to that glass of Nebbiolo, and looking at them is like looking at chalk and cheese. Where the Nebbiolo is pale, the Cabernet is opaque and inky; where the Nebbiolo is brick-red, the Cabernet is a deep, purple-black. They smell different, too. Cabernet, particularly in California, can have an almost exaggerated, essence-like quality, with rich, concentrated aromas of the variety's trademark blackcurrant/cassis characters combined with the tell-tale smoky, vanilla, sweet smells of new French oak barrels in which the wine has been matured for months, sometimes years. Put it in your mouth, though, and you'll find yourself hosting another tannin party – except California Cabernet's tannins are different to those of Piedmont's Nebbiolo: fuller, more mouthfilling, richer, more dense. If drinking Nebbiolo is like walking through a dry forest, drinking California Cabernet can be like walking though dense, damp undergrowth.

TAKE A DEEP BREATH

Does letting a wine "breathe" – or aerating it – really make that much difference? Some wine experts in books and magazines say that breathing doesn't do anything to a wine. Well, the only way to find out is to try it yourself. Take two bottles of the same red wine, preferably a label you're familiar with. Open one a few hours before dinner and decant it into a big, wide-necked jug (this will give it plenty of opportunity to breathe). Open another just before you're ready for dinner. Then pour yourself a glass of both and taste them. Oh, by the way: wine doesn't breathe if you just take the cork out and don't decant it – that's a myth.

WINE 4 & WINE 5: BIG CULT REDS

Barossa Shiraz, McLaren Vale
Shiraz (Australia)

Zinfandel (California)

Carignano, Cannonau
(southern Italy)

Priorato (Cataluna, Spain)

As the craze for bigger and bigger reds has grown, a number of winemakers in both traditional and modern regions have made an effort to make bigger and bigger versions of their existing wines, and, in some cases, have gone back to old styles of big wine that have fallen out of fashion. Because they are usually produced in tiny quantities, and because they have received rave reviews from influential wine critics, these wines have become cult items, selling for sometimes insanely high prices.

In South Australia's warm regions such as McLaren Vale and the Barossa Valley, for example, many growers are using the oldest Shiraz (and/or Grenache) vines they can find, picking their grapes much later than they used to (often with a proportion of the fruit beginning to raisin or shrivel), fermenting in brand-new oak, and extracting as much richness as possible from the grapes. The result is some incredibly dark, heady, rich, and powerful wines with relatively soft acidity, loads of sweet fruit flavour, firm but velvety tannins, and high alcohol. At their best, they are incredibly seductive, hedonistic wines – but subtle they ain't.

Neither, it has to be said, are they unique. You see, other parts of the world have the right combination of old vines, warm climate, innovative winemakers, and rave reviews – places such as Priorato, south of Barcelona on Spain's east coast, for example, where ancient Garnacha (Grenache) vines squeeze out tiny quantities of ultra-ripe, incredibly concentrated fruit, sometimes quite shrivelled, producing alcoholic, massively extracted, powerfully complex, black wines not a million miles in style from the cult Big Reds of California, South Australia, and southern Italy.

IT'S SHOW TIME

You will find that, in many cases, wines that have won gold medals or trophies at wine shows and competitions often turn out to be the bigger styles, with more alcohol, tannin, extract, and flavour. This isn't surprising; despite many wine judges and critics actively seeking to reward the more subtle and delicate styles, when faced with one hundred young reds before lunch, it's hard not to be seduced by the larger styles and the bigger wines – the wines, in other words, that stand out from the crowd. The thing is, these aren't always the best wines to drink with food – unless it's gutsy, char-grilled rib-eye steak, of course (which, apparently, you're not meant to eat every night of the week).

THE ROLE OF THE WINE CRITIC

Just as wine-show judges tend to favour the bigger styles, so some wine critics and wine magazines tend to be top-heavy with their praise of full-bodied, hugely tannic, and oaky red wines. This can lead to a vicious upward spiral: the more oomph a wine has, the higher the scores; the higher the scores, the higher the price; the higher the price, the more status; the more status, the greater demand; the greater the demand, the higher the price – and on it goes. As a result, it sometimes feels as though you have to have particularly deep pockets to follow your passion for Big Wines.

POSH WINES

How come some wines are so much more expensive than others?

So I'm in a taxi, stuck in traffic in the middle of the city, and the driver is telling me about his collection of forty vintages of one of the world's most sought-after and expensive red wines. He's telling me how his cellaring conditions are perfect (high humidity; constant, cool temperature), and how, the last time he cracked open a bottle of the 1971, it was looking a little tired, perhaps past its best.

This comes as a surprise, not because I thought taxi drivers weren't into posh wine (an unfair assumption, obviously), but because posh wines tend to be expensive wines, so the ability to purchase posh wine is usually associated with the ability to pay for it. And, let's face it: taxi drivers seldom appear on the lists of the Top 100 Richest People, right?

Now as it happens, when this particular taxi driver started collecting this particular wine, it was nowhere near as expensive as it is today. Indeed, when the price starting shooting upward – as all top-quality wine prices have done over the last couple of decades – he stopped buying because he couldn't afford it any more. It is, he argues (rather eloquently), only a drink, not a bleedin' status symbol, and besides, there are plenty of other good wines around at more affordable prices.

So why *are* some wines more expensive than others? Does a higher price automatically mean that a wine is better?

WHAT DETERMINES THE PRICE OF A WINE

Well, there are two forces at work here: the actual quality of the wine in the bottle (i.e. the cost of producing it) and the perceived quality, and therefore level of demand (the price someone's willing to pay for it). Actual quality does tend to be related directly to cost. To make great wine, vines must be planted in the best (most expensive) land; yields must be kept low; the best (most expensive) barrels must be used; lesser wine must be left out of the final blend, with just the best used for final bottling, and so on.

A good example of the final price of a wine being dramatically influenced by the cost of production like this is very sweet wines such as Sauternes. Yields are pitifully low, thanks to the shrivelling of the grapes, and the amount of effort, time, and skill involved in the making is incredibly high – thanks to the careful selection of the berries before fermentation.

WHAT YOU SEE ISN'T ALWAYS WHAT YOU GET

Perceived quality, on the other hand, is influenced by less-concrete factors such as good reviews, success at wine competitions, the ability to trade off of the reputation of a region, and the good old-fashioned market forces of supply and demand – none of which are always absolutely related to pure quality. In other words, while many of the world's better wines are deservedly more expensive, not all of them are. There are still many examples of wines that cost a heap of money to make but which are still dreadful and therefore overrated, just as there are examples of wines that have never had a good review and are made in large quantity that are excellent and therefore underrated.

It's important to bear this in mind, because, as I've warned you before, you'll start spending more money than you used to almost as soon as you venture out on this journey called falling love with wine. You'll soon discover that the cheaper wines you once drank don't quite satisfy you as much as the better, and usually more expensive, wines you drink now. But you should always try and look beyond the famous labels, the flashy packaging, the venerable names, and the lofty reputations, and concentrate on the liquid in the glass. That's really the only way to judge quality.

DRINKING TIP: GOING ALL THE WAY

If you've robbed a bank to pay for your great wine, it seems a shame to drink it out of grimy hotel tumblers. Oh, the wine will taste good – great wine always does – but it won't taste as great as it could if you drink it out of fine glassware. I'm not sure you have to get differently shaped glasses for every style of wine you drink (although some people do get that obsessive), but it's worth investing in some good glasses for those special occasions.

VIN DE PAYS

VILLAGE

PREMIER CRU

CHIANT

CHIANTI RISERVA

DRINKING IT

There are two sets of wines to compare and contrast here: three whites demonstrating a steady rise in price (and hopefully, quality), and two reds: one more expensive (and theoretically better) than the other. I have discovered that one of the best ways to find out which is the most preferred wine (although not necessarily the best) is to open them all at once at a table of people eating and talking, don't tell them what the wines are, and see which bottle is emptied first; it's often not the most expensive one. Yes, I know this is a pretty crude technique, but it's honest and it works.

WINE 1: ORDINARY WHITE WINE

EXAMPLES

cheap, commercial styles, blended from several vineyards, such as:

vin de pays **Chardonnay** (southern France)

Riverland Chardonnay (Australia)

The phrase "no frills" will probably pop into your head when you taste this. It looks simple – clear, pale – smells simply of Chardonnay fruit, and tastes simple, pleasant, refreshing, maybe slightly peach-fruity in the mouth. Then again, that's what you want and that's what you get when you don't pay much for a wine: something that tastes nice, that tastes like Chardonnay from high-cropping vineyards fermented simply in stainless steel tanks. Remember, please, that this is hypothetical stuff for the sake of making a point; in reality, some cheap Chardonnay can actually be better than the rather dull drink I've just described – but not a lot better.

WINE 2: SEMI-POSH WHITE WINE

EXAMPLES

mid-price styles from a single, quality region, such as:

Bourgogne Blanc (Burgundy, France)

cool-climate Adelaide Hills Chardonnay (Australia)

Right. You've paid more for this, and the label tells you that you should expect more from it, too – at the very least some kind of regional characters, seeing as it's from a single area (Burgundy, in this case). It looks similar in the glass, but it's much more interesting to smell, with riper, more intense fruit flavour, perhaps some vanilla and savoury oak aromas from some barrel maturation. In the mouth, too, it's got more going for it: it's slightly heavier, thanks to the lower-cropping vineyards, and the flavour lingers longer (a good sign of quality).

WINE 3: POSH WHITE WINE

EXAMPLES

top-quality, expensive styles, such as:

premier cru **burgundy** (France)

single-vineyard Chardonnay from a small producer (Australia)

All bets are off, now. You've just shelled out a small fortune for a pricey white burgundy with some romantic-sounding village name and the words *premier cru* ("first growth") on the label. It had better be bloody good. The colour looks different, for starters: a slightly deeper yellow, perhaps reflecting more barrel influence. And the smells are much more complex: richer, more intense again. It's in the mouth, however, that the quality should leap out at you. If it's worth the money, this will taste more concentrated, finer; it will have more complexity, and a long, lingering aftertaste. Again: remember that this is hypothetical stuff for the sake of making a point. In reality, some expensive Chardonnay can actually be a lot less exciting than the rather lovely drink I've just described.

WINE 4: ORDINARY RED WINE

EXAMPLES

cheap, youngish Chianti (Tuscany, Italy)

cheap Cabernet Sauvignon (Australia, California)

The Chianti wine region in Tuscany is huge, and the grapes that go into the sea of basic red wine sold under the Chianti label are not always the most concentrated, top-quality Sangiovese grapes in the world. Given very little obvious oak treatment, and released quite young, cheap Chianti is designed to be drunk early, so you can appreciate what little of the Sangiovese grape's cherry and berry fruit flavours and grippy, high-acid, tannic structure may have made their way into the wine.

DRINKING TIP: TURN A BLIND EYE

The best way to compare wines honestly is to try them "blind": without knowing their identity. Get a friend to help you here. Take the three white wines featured in this chapter and pour them into three glasses. Now, while you avert your gaze, or have a quick lie-down or something, get your friend to muddle up the order of the wines – remembering which is which, of course. Now come back and taste them, and write down your impressions before finding out the wines' identities.

WINE 5: POSH RED WINE

EXAMPLES

more expensive red from a single district, such as:

Chianti Rufina *riserva*
(Tuscany, Italy)

reserve Cabernet Sauvignon
(Australia, California)

This is a different kettle of grapes altogether. Rufina is a small sub-region of the very large Chianti zone in Tuscany, Italy, located just to the east of Florence, and produces distinctive, much more concentrated, flavourful Sangiovese grapes from lower-yielding vineyards. The word *riserva* on the label indicates that the wine has been selected for its special quality and has spent longer in oak barrels, picking up more savoury complexity to complement the deeper, cherry-fruit flavour. In other words, the extra price should be reflected in higher quality and greater pleasure.

PARTY WINES

The best wines for everyday drinking

I have a way of testing wines for drinkability that is completely unscientific but rigorously realistic. It involves smoke, lots of loud noise, and dogs. Perhaps I should explain. After I've done all the serious wine-writer tasting business – opened a few bottles and poured the wines into good, proper wine glasses, swirled them around, sniffed them and slurped them, thought very hard about them, spat them out, and written down some concise but witty notes in my notebook – I take the wines I like from the tasting out to a barbecue.

I try and make the going as hard as possible for these wines: hot day, lots of smoke and spitting fat, the smells of sausages and steaks and vegetable kebabs emanating from the grill, music blaring from a speaker that's jammed in the open window, kids running around chasing dogs, etc., etc. Then I get some plastic cups and fill them with the wines I thought were pretty good under Serious Wine-tasting Conditions to see how they hold up under Real Wine-drinking Conditions.

If a wine still smells good and tastes good under these conditions, and, importantly, if the bottle is finished quickly – meaning that people are voting with their palates – then I reckon it probably *is* good. If the wine can make people stop halfway through a sentence, look down at their plastic cups, get this expression of pure joy in their eyes and say, "Gee, I like that – what is it?" then I know it's something pretty special indeed.

WHY "EVERYDAY" IS A GOOD WORD

While most of the time the wines that do best in these conditions are the ones with big, obvious flavours, you'd be surprised, actually, how well some of the more delicate styles perform. I'm a strong believer in the idea that a good wine will always manage to convey its quality, no matter

what the drinking vessel, or the food, or the company. I'm also a strong believer that good wine doesn't have to be expensive wine – and, indeed, that everyday drinking wine is usually better if it's moderately priced and of fair, honest quality. Who wants to drink devastatingly expensive, tortuously complex, fine and rare burgundy all the time anyway?

STOCK UP ON THE ESSENTIALS

Buying wine for everyday drinking should be like stocking the kitchen store cupboard. It's an essential part of life to have a few bottles on hand of various wine styles just in case you need them, in the same way that it's essential to have sugar, flour, coffee, tea, and so on available. It's advisable to get a range of wines in, even if you personally don't like something like, maybe, pink wine. It's a safe bet that the next time you decide *not* to buy some fizz, for example, your best friend's sister will drop in, absolutely gasping for a glass of bubbly.

If you think like this, then you'll start looking for the best value when it comes to buying wine – which means thinking seriously about buying by the dozen. Even if you can't afford it yourself, you can always club together with some mates to buy up big. In most cases, bulk purchase means discount, and everybody in your wine-buying syndicate gets to share the cost-saving benefits. This will probably also lead to everybody getting together once you've bought your three-dozen bottles and trying out your wines at a barbecue or some other form of get-together. You're then one step away from forming your very own wine-lovers' commune.

No, I'm kidding about that last sentence (I think...).

DRINKING IT

I've chosen very broad categories of wine here on purpose. Every wine-producing country has its dependable, consistent, party-wine favourites: wines that the locals drink every day without spending too much or thinking too hard. To stop this chapter blowing out too much, however, within each category, I've selected my own personal everyday wines that I like to have on stand-by for unexpected visitors. The great thing about all the wines mentioned in this chapter is that they'll pretty much go with whatever food you can think of – from fiddly, fancy hors d'oeuvres to hot dogs and party pies.

WINE 1: FIZZ

EXAMPLES

cava (Cataluna, Spain)

sparkling Pinot Noir/Chardonnay (Australia, California)

vin mousseaux, **Saumur** (Loire, France)

crémant de Bourgogne (Burgundy, France)

cap classique (South Africa)

What's a party without some bubbly? For my money (and I *would* say this, obviously, being an Australian), the best value for money in the world of sparkling wine is cheap Aussie fizz, preferably made from Pinot Noir and Chardonnay, the classic grapes of Champagne, because it is usually attractively fruity as well as being crisp and bubbly. But any of the many sparkling wines from around the world made by the cheaper methods of production such as tank fermentation will do – as long as they're fresh, clean, and fizzy (*see* "Froth & bubble", page 100, for more on this).

The thing is, you really don't want (or need) to spend too much because (a) people will drink heaps, and (b) you might want to adulterate the wine in some way. I suggest adding a dash of *crème de cassis*, the syrupy, purple, French blackcurrant liqueur, and drinking Kir Royales – very pink, very bubbly, and a whole lot of fun.

PARTY FOOD

The Spaniards have got it right. And the Malaysians. And the Vietnamese. And lots of other cultures, for that matter. Little bites of food, taken often throughout the day, walking through markets, not worrying too hard about the order of a meal, or matching wines specifically to each dish (not that very much food-and-wine matching takes place in your average Penang hawkers' market, mind you, but you get the point).

Given a choice, that's how I'd love to live my life: grazing all day on morsels of delicious food, seasoned liberally with salt and pepper to bring out the flavour of the wines I drink as well as that of food, with a dozen different wines open at once so I can take my pick of whatever I feel like whenever I feel like it. That'd be great. But it's an impossible dream. I'd never get anything done, and I'd blow up like a balloon after a couple of days.

DRINKING TIPS FOR PARTY ANIMALS

Here are some common-sense tips to serving wine at a party:

☿ Buy some beer as well, and some soft drinks. It's hard to believe, I know, but not everybody likes wine.

☿ You can't have a party without a big crate (or your bath) full of ice. Sorry, but you can't – I mean, where are you going to keep the beers?

☿ If you need to chill wine quickly, the best thing to do is to plunge the bottle in a bucket half-filled with ice, half with cold water that's got a handful or two of salt dissolved in it. The salty brine chills down to a lower temperature than water's freezing point, so the solution cools your bottle quicker.

☿ Buy some more beer.

☿ Keep your red wines cool in hot weather, in the ice if need be, especially if you're partying outside. There's nothing more horrible than Cabernet drunk at blood temperature, and I mean *nothing* more horrible.

☿ Put ice-cubes and soda water in your white wine if you want a more refreshing drink.

☿ If you're partying in winter, on the other hand, try making mulled wine: warm a couple of bottles' worth of soft, cheap red in a saucepan, add some cinnamon sticks and a clove-studded orange, and maybe a star anise or two. What you don't drink you can sweeten to taste with brown sugar and use to poach some pears.

☿ Don't forget the beer.

WINE 2: WHITE WINE

WHAT TO LOOK FOR

aromatic, flavourful, salad- and fish-friendly wines like Riesling and Sauvignon Blanc (from practically anywhere); as well as crowd-pleasing, fairly neutral, unwooded Italian whites, such as Frascati and Orvieto that everyone will be happy with; or you could just buy Chardonnay….

I know that at most parties these days, wherever you are in the world, everybody seems to serve and drink and be quite happy with the ubiquitous Chardonnay. And so many varietally labelled Chardonnays at the cheaper end of the price spectrum seem to fit the bill, too, regardless of whether they're from the Cape, California, or Chile. But I'd much rather drink something aromatic and unwooded, with a bit of positive varietal verve and grape character – like Riesling or Sauvignon Blanc, two wines that can taste really good out of plastic cups, if they're cold enough. On the other hand, I've found that when you've got a group of people together with sometimes disparate tastes in wine, the best bet is to go for something that's not going to offend anybody – like well-made, clean, fruity (but not too fruity) Italian white wine.

WINE 3: PINK WINE

EXAMPLES

rosado (Navarra, Spain)

Grenache rosé, Shiraz rosé
(South Australia)

**Bandol rosé, Côtes de Provence
rosé, Côtes de Lubéron rosé,
Gigondas rosé** (France)

Pink, or rosé, wines are great, because they taste lovely with just about any kind of food you care to mention, from delicate Japanese sushi to hefty, garlicky Mediterranean roast lamb. The best are made by crushing ripe, red grapes and leaving the juice in contact with the skins to leach out the red colour for only a few hours before being pressed off to finish fermentation in a tank. What you end up with is a pink wine. (The worst are made by adding a bit of ordinary red wine to some even more ordinary white wine – but we don't need to concern ourselves with them here.) The examples I've given are also all quite gutsy and on the dry side, so they sit perfectly between white and red wine in terms of weight and user-friendliness (sweeter pink wines tend to taste quite cloying as they warm up in the glass).

One very important thing to consider, though, is that you should, on the whole, drink pink wine as young as possible – preferably up to about twelve months after the vintage, while it's still fresh and vibrant.

WINE 4: RED WINE

EXAMPLES

Côtes du Rhône (France)

Chinon (Loire, France)

Minervois (southern France)

Chianti (Tuscany, Italy)

Barbera, Dolcetto (north-west Italy)

Grenache/Shiraz (Australia)

cheap Merlot (California, Washington State)

All right, all right. If I'm being absolutely honest here, I love to bring out the big guns at barbecues and other parties: the black, strapping, rich, and powerful wines I wrote about in "Tall, Dark, & Handsome" (page 74). But also, to tell the truth, I can't afford these wines very often, and most people are more than happy with medium-bodied and lighter-bodied reds like the examples I've given. Reds that emphasize bright, varietal, and regional fruit flavours, moderate to soft tannins, and little or no obvious oak-maturation characters. Red wine like this – easy for most people to drink – is also the best all-rounder when it comes to food, especially in a party situation. I've been ecstatically happy eating barbecued white fish with a young Chianti (a match you wouldn't normally expect to work) because the company and the mood and the music were so good, and I didn't pay the slightest bit of attention to any slight flavour clashes on my tongue, enjoying, instead, the wonderful combination of everything.

BUYING TIPS

To become a really canny buyer of wine bargains, you might want to pick up some of the following habits.

♉ **Start reading.** Yes, I know I have a vested interest in you reading more wine-writing (especially my books – plug, plug), but I really do think that by becoming better informed, you will be able to make better buying decisions.

♉ **Be a pest.** Make sure your local wine shop knows you're passionate about your booze, and encourage the staff to let you know in advance of any specials or bargains that might be coming up.

♉ **Taste, taste, taste.** Go to as many tastings and wine expos as possible. It's here that you'll pick up some useful snippets and recommendations.

♉ **Get off your bum.** Visit wine regions. Yes, I know; this may not be all that easy if you're a few hundred kilometres and several large expanses of water away from your closest vineyard, but nobody ever said life was meant to be easy. You'll learn more at the cellar door than you will reading books. It's as simple as that.

♉ **Don't believe the hype.** Don't be taken in by gold-medal stickers, glowing reviews, and lofty reputations. Use them as a guide, by all means, but always rely ultimately on your own tastes and preferences.

FROTH & BUBBLE
What makes sparkling wine so special?

Here's a quick quiz to make sure you're still awake and paying attention this far into the book. There is one thing common to all the following snapshots of life; what is it? The launch of a ship. The winning podium at the Grand Prix. Your wedding/birthday/christening. Your horse coming in first. Winston Churchill. Candlelit dinner for two. James Bond seducing Pussy Galore. The common theme is, of course, sparkling wine – or, to be more precise, Champagne.

For the last couple of centuries, fizzy wine has been the number-one drink of choice all over the world when it comes to celebrating anything. Imagine, for example, toasting the bride and groom with a heavy, sweet vintage port. Just doesn't work, does it? Along with this sense of celebration also comes a hefty price tag. Champagne is still undoubtedly the vinous symbol of luxury, with some of the well-known top Champagne producers (or *grand marques* as they're called) enjoying household-name recognition in households that could never actually afford to buy the stuff. So why do we love sparkling wine so much? And why is the best bubbly – which comes from the Champagne region in northern France – so damned expensive?

WHY BUBBLES COST THE WAY THEY DO

Well, a lot of the expense has to do with the cost of production. Bubbly is an incredibly labour- and time-intensive wine to make. Champagnes, together with the best sparkling wines in countries such as Australia, the USA, and New Zealand, are made in the following way, using the so-called *méthode champenoise*, or "Champagne method".

It works likes this. White Chardonnay and red Pinot Noir grapes (and often some red Pinot Meunier grapes) from cool-climate vineyards are picked while they still have high levels of acid: a little less ripe than they would be if they were being turned into non-sparkling wine. The grapes are pressed very gently, and the clear juice is fermented to form a very light, dry wine.

This light, tart, pale wine is blended together with lots of other light, tart, pale wines from different vineyards, each with slightly different flavour and taste attributes to create complexity, and this "base wine" is then put into those familiar heavy Champagne bottles with a little sugar and a little yeast. The wine is sealed (usually with something called a "crown seal", or beer-bottle cap) and laid down in a cool cellar.

The yeast soon starts working on the sugar and fermenting it, producing a little more alcohol and lots of that wonderful by-product of fermentation, carbon dioxide. Because the bottle is tightly sealed, however, the carbon dioxide can't escape and so it sits there, dissolved in the wine as carbonic acid, waiting for someone to open the bottle and let it literally erupt into the atmosphere.

WHAT HAPPENS NEXT

After the secondary fermentation has finished in the bottle, the wine continues to sit quietly in its cool cellar, because as the dead yeast cells (the "lees", remember?) inside the bottle begin to break down over months through a process called autolysis, they contribute a bready, floral, distinctive aroma and taste to the wine.

Each bottle is then gently shaken and inverted, so that the sludgey lees sediment slips down into the neck of the bottle; this process is called "riddling". The bottle necks are then dipped in freezing brine, so that the plug of frozen wine and sediment shoots out of the bottle when the cap is opened, without too much of the wine escaping; this process is called "disgorging". Each bottle is then topped up with a little wine and sugar (to balance the sometimes aggressive acidity of the wine), then quickly re-sealed with the familiar cork, wire, and foil before the fizz escapes.

Because of the high cost of production, Champagne has always been the preserve of the historically (or suddenly) rich, a situation that the winemakers of Champagne (the Champenois) have capitalized on and enhanced through centuries of very smart marketing. The thing is, the Champenois have done such a good job of inflating the image of "the real thing" (French Champagne, from the Champagne region), that all sparkling wine – even the bargain-basement stuff with plastic corks on special in your local supermarket – has the feeling of special occasion about it. I reckon it has something to do with the bubbles, too: not just the old romantic idea that they look like stars, but also the idea – whether it's true or not – that the carbon dioxide helps the alcohol get into your bloodstream faster.

DRINKING IT

OK, I know it seems strange to start this chapter by drinking a sweet wine, but I want you to try something that reflects the very first examples of sweet wine that were made before the *méthode champenoise* was perfected, roughly 300 years ago. We'll then go on to some examples of wines that are made using that method, from simple, everyday fizz to a couple of very special drops. If you're feeling especially gregarious and hospitable, you may want to invite some friends over and get in a couple of tubs of caviar to accompany this chapter's wines. Then again, you may prefer to indulge alone.

WINE 1: SWEET SPARKLING WINE

EXAMPLE

Moscato d'Asti (north-west Italy)

The first sparkling wines ever drunk by our distant forbears would have tasted a bit like Moscato. To make it, ripe Moscato (Muscat) grapes are picked, crushed, pressed, and fermented in a large tank, but halfway through fermentation – when only half the sugar has been converted into alcohol, and while the carbon dioxide is still being produced – the wine is filtered and bottled under pressure. The result is gently, naturally foaming wine with a natural grapey sweetness and only about five per cent alcohol. This is why I say it tastes like a very old-style wine; you can imagine the very first amateur *vignerons* playing with fermentation, becoming impatient, and just guzzling the half-fermented, sweet, sherbety liquid as soon as they could (in the same way I'm inclined to guzzle the stuff in summer).

DRINKING TIP: DON'T BE TOO COOL

Most people serve sparkling wine – and most white wines, for that matter – too cold, as if they were serving an icy, frosty, Australian lager. You certainly want the wine to be cold (try opening a warm bottle of fizz and you'll find the wine gushing out in a stream), but if it's too cold, you'll kill the delicate flavours. Think of cooling your fizz by chilling it in a trickling stream. If you haven't got a stream handy, try half an hour in an ice bucket.

DRINKING TIP: BUBBLY FOOD

For me, the traditional aphrodisiac accompaniment to bubbly – oysters – just doesn't work all that often (certainly not in a gastronomic sense). I find that, unless the bubbly is really flavourful (like a *blanc de noirs*), the oysters just overpower it. I like more delicate food with my fizz (especially pink fizz), and the best of all is salmon – smoked, sushi, pan-fried, air-cured – or trout. Another good match is sweeter Champagne or *méthode champenoise* with pâté and rich *charcuterie*. I'm not one of those zealots, however, who drinks Champagne all the way through the meal, or insists that Parmesan ice-cream with shaved black truffle is the best accompaniment (and I didn't make that up, honest).

CHEAP FIZZ

The *méthode champenoise,* or *traditionelle,* as you've seen, is time-consuming and costly, but most people can't wait that long and are not prepared to pay that much. So winemakers have developed cheaper, quicker techniques to turn still wine fizzy.

♀ Transfer method: the procedure is followed in almost exactly the same way as for Champagne, except for riddling and disgorging. Instead, the wine is transferred from all of the bottles into a big pressure tank, where the sediment is filtered out, and the clear, fizzy wine is bottled, also under pressure.

♀ Tank method: instead of taking place in individual bottles, the secondary fermentation takes place in a big pressure tank before the wine is filtered and bottled. Because there is little or no extended contact with the lees and therefore no autolysis, tank-method wines are invariably less complex and expensive than transfer- or traditional-method wines.

♀ The soft-drink method: the very cheapest way of making bubbly is simply to inject carbon dioxide into a tank of base wine. You can easily tell carbonated wine because it's usually cheap, the bubbles are coarse, and they disappear quickly – unlike the bubbles in a traditional-method wine, for example, which are tiny and persistent.

WINE 2: NON-VINTAGE SPARKLING WINE

EXAMPLES

non-vintage Champagne (France)
méthode traditionelle (France)
traditional method sparkling (Australia, New Zealand, the USA)
cap classique (South Africa)

The majority of production in the region of Champagne is non-vintage wine that is a blend of more than one year. In other countries, such as Australia and New Zealand, vintage-dated fizz is much more common, and the non-vintage stuff is usually quite cheap. Blending is the key to almost all Champagne production: blending of the long-tasting, lemony Chardonnay grapes with the rounder, more savoury-tasting Pinot Noir grapes, and the honeyed, earthy Pinot Meunier grapes. Blending of the wines from many different vineyards creates complexity in the single base wine; and blending wines from more than one year creates consistency, with the lighter, cooler, vintage wines balancing the richer, warmer, vintage wines (*see* more on this in "Fiddling Around", page 56).

WINE 3: VINTAGE SPARKLING WINE

EXAMPLES

vintage Champagne (France)

vintage-dated, traditional method sparkling (Australia, New Zealand, the USA)

Vintage-dated wine is only made by the better producers in the best years in Champagne (six out of every ten, say), when the grapes have enough complexity and quality to stand up on their own two feet without having to be supported by wines blended from different years. As a result, vintage Champagne is usually more expensive than non-vintage Champagne – although some *grand marques* have a non-vintage wine as their flagship, and some take the specialness of vintage to extremes by releasing a single-vineyard wine (which is usually hyper-expensive). Other sparkling wine styles are *blanc de blancs*, made solely from Chardonnay and usually quite fine and delicate; *blanc de noirs*, made solely from Pinot Noir and Pinot Meunier and usually weightier, richer, and more full-on; *demi-sec* (medium-dry); *doux* and *riche* (both sweet); and *crémant* (softer, creamier fizz).

THE NUN'S FART

The best way to open a bottle of sparkling wine is not with a bang, but a whimper. Take off the foil, slowly undo the wire and loosen it, but leave it on. Now grip the cork and wire with one hand, and grip the bottom of the bottle with the other. Slowly turn the bottle, and prize the cork out gently: the sound you want to hear is "pffft!" (like a nun's fart – snigger, snigger). This way, you won't lose too much of the precious gas that the winemaker has gone to so much trouble putting into the bottle in the first place.

THE MAGIC FLUTE

Sparkling wine is the only style I get very bossy about in terms of glassware; you simply have to use long, tall, narrow flute glasses, so that, again, the bubbles don't escape too quickly and you get to watch them effervesce in your glass. Those wide-mouthed, shallow glasses (famously modelled on Marie Antoinette's breasts) are useless for fizz; save them for chocolate mousse. Whichever glass you use, however, make sure it's free from detergent residue or dirt or grease of any kind; otherwise, your wine simply won't be fizzy after you've poured it.

WHAT'S IN A NAME?

Of all the traditional European wine names that other countries' winemakers have adopted over the centuries – names such as "Claret", "Sherry" or "Hock" – "Champagne" is the one that is most fiercely protected. As a result, most countries have agreed to stop using the name on labels of their sparkling wine, and you'd be unlikely to find an Australian or Chilean "Champagne" these days.

WINE 4: PINK FIZZ

EXAMPLES

rosé Champagne (France)

traditional method sparkling rosé (Australia, New Zealand, the USA)

Given a choice, I would probably drink pink Champagne over all the other styles. Maybe I'm just an incurable romantic, or maybe it's because pink fizz tends to go much better with food – and I'm usually eating when I'm drinking. There are two basic ways to make fizz pink: either add a little red wine to the blend before secondary fermentation (the final wine will be more of an orangey, onion-skin colour), or add a little after disgorging (the final wine will be more of a pale pink, or salmon colour). Because of the addition of some red wine, I find pink fizz often has a touch more body and complexity. Drink a bottle that's also been cellared for a while and you can get some incredible, ethereal, almost decadent flavours.

Many countries also make a sparkling red wine by putting fuller-bodied red base wines through the traditional method (for more on this, *see* "Altered States", page 123).

PENSIONED OFF
Does all wine get better with age?

My hands are trembling. I don't believe it: my hands are trembling. All I'm doing is opening a bottle of wine, for God's sake, but I'm filled with nervous anticipation, like I'm on a first date or something. Then again, the wine in question *is* a bit special. It's a couple of decades old, the bottle is covered in dust (the way all older wines should be), and I paid a barrow-load of cash for it, so I'm kind of expecting that it's going to taste bloody fantastic.

I'm also trembling because the last time I had this particular old red, it really was amazing. It made me sit dead still, slowly sipping its wondrous richness, taking reverential sniffs of its impossibly complex aromas. And I'm hoping – praying – that this bottle tastes as good.

Old wine has this aura about it. Since Roman times, a wine's ability to develop and get better in the bottle (or the amphora, in those days) was seen as one of the major attributes of greatness. And while I love drinking wines young, with all their bold, primary, varietal fruit flavours, there's no doubt that the best wines I've ever drunk in my life have been mature examples: five, ten, twenty years old or more.

WHAT IT TAKES TO MATURE

Not every wine gets better with age. Indeed, some (or most, even) are designed and made to be drunk within the first twelve months of their lives – before the next vintage comes around, in fact. But a minority of wines have the right combination of factors to ensure that they do develop and change for the better in the bottle.

With any wine (white, red, still or sparkling, sweet), the most important ageing factor is acidity. Generally, the higher the acidity, the longer a wine will age, which is partly why old German Rieslings and

Loire Valley Chenin Blancs from the nineteenth century are still deliciously youthful: both these varieties are high in acid. Sweet white wines also have a propensity to age well, because behind all that sugar there's often a good whack of acidity.

With red wines, the other main attribute for ageworthiness is tannin. A good level of robust tannin in a young red wine will act as both preservative and taste component as the wine sits in its bottle over many years. Alcohol in all styles also acts as a preservative, which is one of the reasons fortified wines can age for decades in both barrel and bottle.

WHAT AGEING DOES TO A WINE

The ageing process itself is one where the various components of the wine – alcohol; acids; flavour and structure compounds leached from the grape skins and oak barrels during maturation; dissolved oxygen – slowly combine over time to form new compounds, or new flavours, and new tastes. As the tannins and colour compounds in red wines age, for example, they polymerize, forming larger and larger molecules, until eventually they fall out of solution, making the wine a lighter colour, and creating the crusty sediment at the bottom of the bottle.

If you're interested in seeing how wines develop as they age, then you'll either have to buy them pre-aged (from auction, say – which can be frighteningly expensive), or lay them down yourself. And this means providing as many of the right cellaring conditions as possible. The best cellar will have a cool temperature (about 15°C/59°F), a constant temperature (rapid heating and cooling makes the corks expand and shrink, letting air get to the wine and spoiling it), darkness (too much light can affect wine in clear glass bottles), and good humidity of about seventy-five per cent so that the corks don't dry out. That last bit is also the reason why bottles are stored on their sides: so that the corks are kept moist by the constant contact with the liquid inside.

However, don't worry too much if you can't find all these things in one place. A constant, not-so-cool temperature is better than a place that gets very cold and very hot from day to night (although bear in mind that the warmer the average temperature, the more rapid any flavour development will be, and the cooler, the slower).

Also, don't worry too much about perfect cellaring conditions if you're only keeping your wine for a year or two. Even during this short time, you will still be able to taste changes in flavour and taste: something I'd recommend for cheaper and medium-priced wines.

DRINKING IT

The problem with wine books is that they tend to go out of date pretty much as soon as they hit the shelves. This is a pretty good thing for us wine writers, because we're kept busy updating them. As a result, if you're reading this in, say, 2010 (assuming it's still in print, and assuming people are still reading books by then), the vintages I've given as examples will obviously bear little relation to what's available. But I reckon that it shouldn't be too hard for a smart person like you to extrapolate the idea and choose vintages that correspond to the point I'm trying to make. You'll see what I mean if you read on....

WINE 1: YOUNG WHITE WINE

WHAT TO LOOK FOR

one of the best wines you could drink to illustrate how whites age is Semillon from the Hunter Valley in New South Wales, Australia; look for a recent vintage – perhaps 2001

During it's first twelve months or so, most white wine is fairly pale – almost water-white in some cases – with perhaps some flashes of green. Young Hunter Semillon is almost always unwooded, and it is usually quite pale. It smells fresh and clean and slightly lemony, even grassy: these are typical smells for the grape variety. And, because it's often low in alcohol (ten or eleven per cent), it is light, even quite ineffectual in the mouth, with crisp, chalky acidity. Indeed, when it's young, Hunter Semillon can really be quite unexciting (dull, even) and it sometimes makes you wonder why it has survived for so long and become such a popular wine style. The answer, of course, lies in its ageworthiness. Give it ten years of undisturbed rest in a cool cellar and it transforms from a caterpillar into a butterfly.

WINE 2: OLDER WHITE WINE

WHAT TO LOOK FOR

a Hunter Semillon from the same region (same producer, preferably) as the 2001 wine you've just tried, but from the 1991 vintage

It's hard to believe this started life as the wine I've just described. Glowing yellow in colour (thanks to the deepening in hue caused by gradual oxidation), smelling of freshly buttered toast and lime syrup, this white wine has amazing complexity and a richness of flavour, but then finishes dry and light, thanks to its low alcohol content. Incredibly, as is the case in many other bottle-aged, unwooded white wines, the smells and flavours in this are so vanilla- and toast-like that you would swear the wine has been fermented or aged in a new-oak barrel. It hasn't, but that's the magic of bottle-age: it gives the wine a whole new layer of sometimes evocative flavours that are a world away from the simple flavours of fruit and winemaking.

DRINKING TIP: THE LINE-UP

Some people reckon that if you're trying wines across a range of vintages, then drinking young wines before old wines is the way to go. The young wines, they argue, are more simple, while the older wines are more complex. Some people, on the other hand, like to drink older wines first, because they tend to be more subtle and can be drowned out by the boldness of a younger wine. You need to try it both ways to work out which suits you best (as the actress said to the bishop). Whichever way you decide to go, however, bear in mind that young wines tend to stand up better to bolder, fuller-flavoured food, while older wines, being more subtle and more developed, need more subtle food.

OLD AND CRUSTY

Decanting a wine is particularly recommended if the wine in question is old and red, although very old whites can benefit from it, too. The bottle will probably contain bits of sediment which are harmless but not terribly pleasant to crunch on or get stuck between your teeth, and it makes sense to separate the wine from the gunk. To decant, stand the wine up for a few hours first so that all the sediment falls to the bottom of the bottle. Then get a clean jug (or fancy crystal decanter if you really must), and, standing over a light of some kind (candle if you're romantic, upturned torch if you're practical), slowly pour the wine into the jug in one clean motion, stopping just before the sediment gets to the neck – you can watch for this by looking down at the light through the bottle.

SURE THINGS FOR THE CELLAR

Here's a list of just a few personal favourites that I know will develop well in the cellar (not that I can bear to keep my hands off them for long enough). The time in parentheses is how long I'd suggest keeping them: i.e. how long they'll develop well. Bear in mind, however, that these are all consciously conservative estimates, as I'd rather drink something too young than too old.

- ♀ Top-quality sparkling white or red wine (five years)
- ♀ Riesling, particularly German and Australian (ten years or more)
- ♀ Australian Semillon (ten years)
- ♀ White burgundy (ten years)
- ♀ Red Bordeaux (fifteen years)
- ♀ Red northern Rhône wines (ten years)
- ♀ California Cabernet and Merlot (fifteen years)
- ♀ Italian reds: Barolo, Barbaresco, Amarone, Brunello (ten years)
- ♀ Australian Shiraz (fifteen years)
- ♀ Spanish reds like Rioja (ten years)
- ♀ Vintage port (twenty years)

WINES 3, 4, & 5: YOUNG, MIDDLE-AGED, & OLDER RED WINE

WHAT TO LOOK FOR

firm, tannic reds, such as Bordeaux or another Cabernet-based blend, and find a young one (2000 vintage, perhaps), a slightly older one (a five-year-old: perhaps 1995) and a mature one (say, a ten-year-old – 1990); all same or similar wine

I want you to line up three glasses and pour a bit from each bottle. See immediately how they differ in colour? The young wine is a deep, purple-red; the middle wine is beginning to look more garnet/ruby-coloured; the older wine is beginning to fade and brown a little. Again, this colour change is partly a result of controlled oxidation. They smell different, too, these wines. The young wine has obvious fruit smells (blackcurrant, that type of thing) and some raw-oak smells (toast, wood); the middle wine's fruit is beginning to soften, and the oak is turning more savoury and mellow; and the older wine is beginning to pick up an array of mature smells such as leather, macerated fruit, and earth. In the mouth, the main and most noticeable difference is in how the tannin feels. It's quite raw, powdery, and assertive in the young wine, beginning to soften and lengthen in the middle wine, and is mellow, firm, and lingering in the older wine. As the wines get older, too, there should be more complexity, more subtlety, and more finesse.

CORK UNDER SIEGE

You will have noticed the increasing use of non-cork seals on bottles of wine you buy: plastic corks, screw-caps, etc. On the whole, this has come about because of the high incidence of cork taint (see "Altered States", page 116, for more on this). But there are two side effects of these changes. For a start, wines bottled with plastic corks often oxidize after twelve months, while, more encouragingly, wines bottled under screw-caps – particularly light, aromatic white wines – age far more reliably and slowly than wines bottled under cork.

ALTERED STATES
The world's more unusual wines

Some wines freak me out. No, seriously. I'll open a bottle, pour myself a glass, take a quick peek at it to make sure it's not full of sediment or a disgusting brown colour, and then I'll put the glass to my nose, expecting to smell wine and – *whoomph!* Suddenly, my nostrils will be filled with smells I have never smelled before: smells I never thought it possible to find in fermented grape juice.

Or I'll take a sniff and the wine will smell okay – like wine at least, with kind of vinous fruit smells, and some lift from the alcohol, perhaps, and a hint of vanilla from the oak-ageing or whatever. Then I'll innocently put the wine in my mouth and – *whaaack*! The liquid will immediately do the strangest things to my tongue, tasting like no taste I ever tasted before: tastes that I never thought it possible to find in fermented grape juice!

Far from being put off, however, I become intrigued. I soon realized when I got into this wine game that there are a whole heap of wines that are made in such bizarre ways, from such obscure grape varieties, in such unexpected places, that you can begin to develop a weird desire to try them. In fact, in my case, this desire has become an obsession – a fetish, almost – and I can't wait to discover the next weird and wonderful, kooky wine. Some people like to push themselves to the edge of their physical limits in extreme sports. Some people like to seek out and eat extreme foods: fish that can kill you, reptile bile, endangered insects. I'm happy drinking extreme wines. I reckon it's probably safer, for one thing.

Many of the world's weirder wines are wonderfully old-fashioned – relics, if you like, of a time when grape varieties and winemaking techniques were highly regionalized, and practised alongside equally regionalized cultural and culinary traditions. For example, variations of dried-grape wines are made all over the traditional wine-producing world, harking back to a time before modern viticultural practices like canopy management and fungicide and pesticide sprays. Back then, the only way to get lots of sugar and flavour in your wine was to cut the grapes off the vine and shrivel them in the sun before fermentation.

There are wines that exploit the unique growing conditions of where they're made: botrytis-affected wines that love the cool, damp autumns in temperate regions; wines that are made from easily dried grapes in warm, sunny regions; wines made from frozen grapes in very cold regions; wines that are sometimes literally cooked in hot regions. There are wines that are echoes, too, of fashions and styles that have long since passed. And there are many strange and wonderful wines out there that take advantage of wine's propensity to oxidize, turning this into a positive rather than negative thing by controlling the rate and manner of oxidation.

"A" IS FOR ANTI-GLOBALIZATION...

The good thing about all these wines is the fact that, in most cases, they are still highly regionalized, and therefore offer an excellent, characterful alternative to the oceans of internationally styled, "safe", user-friendly wines floating around on supermarkets shelves all over the globe. Bored with yet another sweet, plush, oaky Syrah that tastes as though it could have come from Australia, even though it was made in California? Then try a rich, sweet, powerful, purple sparkling Shiraz that could only have come from Australia. Tired of boring, flabby Chilean Chardonnay? Then try a searingly acidic, totally individual Txakoli from the Basque coast of northern Spain, made from the local Hondarrabi Zuri and Munemahatsa grape varieties: perfect with the local seafood. Actually, no; that might be quite difficult, as hardly any of the tiny production of Txakoli is exported. But that's precisely my point.

These wines are like the thousands of ancient, highly localized languages and cultures that are in danger of disappearing from around the world. They sound exotic, they are often hard to understand, but if you make the effort to appreciate them, they can be incredibly rewarding. Problem is, like the ancient and varied languages of the world, these wines are in danger of disappearing, too, as people are increasingly content to use the vinous equivalents of "global" languages like English (or, to be more accurate, *American* English).

AMARONE ICE WINE SPARKLING SHIRAZ MADEIRA

DRINKING IT

I'm going to be upfront with you here: finding some of these wines may be difficult. In some cases, they are produced in such small quantities that availability is limited. In most cases, they are simply so unusual, and therefore not to everybody's taste, that many wine merchants may not stock them. This is where making friends with your wine merchant comes in handy: you may be able to convince him or her to get some wines in especially for you. You may also have to do some digging, by searching on the internet or phoning around; but then the thrill of the hunt is part of the pleasure of finding these wines.

WINE 1: SHRIVELLED WINE

WHAT TO LOOK FOR

wines made from dried grapes, such as:

amarone, recioto (Veneto, Italy)
passito (Italy)

There's something wonderfully medieval about wines made from dried grapes. In the case of *amarone* wines, made in the Valpolicella region of the Veneto in Italy, ripe Corvina, Molinara, and Rondinella grapes are picked and then laid out on mats, or hung from beams and rafters in specially designed warehouses. Over a period of months, the grapes begin to shrivel and dry out, becoming slightly infected with the "noble rot" known as botrytis (normally associated with sweet wines). The shrivelled grapes are then fermented, and the combination of high sugar, dried flavours, and botrytis produces a wine that is deep, rich, raisiny, alcoholic (fifteen per cent or so), and incredibly powerful. Recioto della Valpolicella is a sweeter, sometimes slightly fizzy version of the same wine; you'll also find the words *recioto* and *passito* on some Italian sweet white wines (Recioto di Soave, for example, and Passito di Pantelleria), indicating that the grapes have been raisined before being fermented. These wines are not common, but are often sensationally intense and sweet.

DRINKING TIP: UNUSUAL FOOD

It would be too obvious, wouldn't it, to recommend weird food with these weird wines – but that's precisely what I'm going to do (nobody ever accused me of being subtle). You can't go past weird cheese if you want a really way-out taste experience, and, as it happens, cheese is often a particularly good match for the unusual wines listed in this chapter. Look for those wonderfully weird cheeses from Spain and Corsica and other Mediterranean countries, that have exceptional blue mould, are wrapped in sycamore leaves, or rolled in wild herbs plucked from rugged hillsides. Cheeses, in other words, that are equally as old-fashioned, intensely flavoured, and proudly regional as the wines.

UNEXPECTED PLACES

As well as wines made in unusual ways, I like looking for wines made in places you wouldn't normally associate with wine production: the tannic red wines made from Tannat in Uruguay, for example, or the sparkling wine made in India, or the increasing number of wines coming out of China's vast vineyards. All of these signal hope for an always interesting future of wine drinking. Who knows where the next great wines will come from?

WINE 2: EXTREME WINE

WHAT TO LOOK FOR

sweet white wines made from naturally frozen grapes, such as:

Eiswein (Austria, Germany)

ice wine (Canada)

In the very, very cool vineyards of Germany, some Riesling grapes can often hang on the vine way after all the others have been picked, sometimes right into the depths of winter, when snow and frost can shroud the vineyards in a cloak of magical white. If this happens (and it doesn't happen every year – only if the conditions are right and the grapes are healthy), the water content of the grapes can partially freeze, concentrating the sugar and acid immensely. If these grapes are picked and crushed while still frozen, the resulting syrup makes some of the most unbelievably intense, sweet white wine in the universe: wine that still manages to retain its fragrance and varietal complexity. As you can imagine, such wines are horrendously expensive and rare. Luckily, some cheeky New World producers have taken a radical short cut and make their ice wine out of grapes that have been picked and stuck into a freezer. It's not as good, but it's a damn sight cheaper.

SOME OTHER UNUSUAL WINES

Here's a list of some of the world's more esoteric wines.

♈ *Vin santo* (Italy). The whole catastrophe of weird winemaking techniques is thrown at *vin santo*, or "holy wine": it is made from local Tuscan white grapes, dried on mats before being fermented to varying levels of sweetness, and then aged, often for years, in old barrels in warm rooms, without topping up – so an element of sherry-like oxidation is introduced to the mix. *Vin santo* can be very dry or very sweet, and it's hard to tell which before you open the bottle.

♈ *Vin de paille* (France). Literally, "straw wine", *vin de paille* is made in tiny quantities in the Rhône Valley and the Jura, from white grapes that have been left to dry on straw mats before being fermented in a similar fashion to the *recioto* and *passito* wines of Italy.

♈ Banyuls and Maury (France). Intense, sweet, fortified red wines made from ultra-ripe, sometimes vine-shrivelled Grenache grapes in south-west France, these are not dissimilar to vintage port. Both of these French wines, however, can often spend a long, long time in barrel and pick up more sherry-like, or *rancio*, characters.

♈ Gouais (Australia). Gouais is a grape variety that is so dull it has been banned in France, but it still exists in a couple of vineyards in Australia. Recent research reveals that it is one of the parent vines (along with Pinot Noir) of Chardonnay.

♈ Cordon cut (Australia). A variation of a very old technique used to make sweet wines in Europe, where the fruit-bearing canes are cut from the main trunk of the vine, and the grapes are left to hang on the trellis wire, shrivelling and intensifying.

♈ Tokáji Eszencia (Hungary). This incredibly rich, syrupy, slightly alcoholic, unbelievably rare wine is made from the sticky juice that runs from highly botrytized grapes waiting to be crushed and made into Tokáji Aszú, the more common form of sweet, orange-coloured, honeyed wine from this part of the world.

♈ Samos Nectar (Greece). Similar in style to Eszencia, but made from very ripe Muscat grapes grown in the hillside vineyards of the Greek island of Samos, then dried before being made into wine. Like Eszencia and many other dried-grape wines, it can develop in barrel and bottle for decades.

♈ Retsina (Greece). Made by adding small chunks of pine to the fermenting white wine. It is an extremely old wine style; the ancient Romans often added resin (among other things) to their wines.

WINE 3: SURREAL WINE

WHAT TO LOOK FOR

sparkling red wines; and forget bog-standard, cheap-and-cheerful Lambrusco, look for the good stuff, such as:

Lambrusco Reggiano (Italy)

sparkling Shiraz (Australia)

In the late nineteenth century, sparkling wine didn't just come from Champagne and wasn't only dry. If it could have bubbles in it, it did have, and wine drinkers from London to New York to Sydney were tucking into sweet sparkling hock and red sparkling burgundy – not to mention sparkling claret. In Australia, the local winemakers made their sparkling "burgundy" out of ripe, rich Shiraz, and put the grapes through the full *méthode traditionelle* secondary-fermentation rigmarole.

The result is a wonderfully idiosyncratic style that persists to this day: deep-purple in colour, with often bright-pink foaming bubbles; rich, ripe, and berry-like flavours; full, soft, and often quite sweet in the mouth, it's a style that is served cold – preferably on hot days at a barbecue, with something really meaty, like venison or lamb, sizzling away on the grill. Wine snobs reckon sparkling Shiraz is just a fun wine, not worthy of serious consideration. I reckon it's one of the best wines in the world, and an exceptional match for a range of foods – especially sweet-roasted Peking duck.

LOOKING FOR QUALITY ON THE LABEL

Most of the traditional wine countries have legally regulated phrases on the label indicating quality. France's *appellation controlée*, for example, tells you that the wine comes from a (theoretically) superior region, while Germany's ascending quality scale relates in part to the ripeness of the grapes when they were picked: *Kabinett*, *Spätlese*, *Auslese*, *Beerenauslese*, and *Trockenbeerenauslese*. These are, however, only indications of quality; you can never automatically assume that the wine inside the bottle will be good or worth the money (in both – most – cases, the reputation of the producer is often a better guide to quality). Neither can you assume that unregulated words such as "reserve" and "old vine" guarantee quality in countries such as Australia and the USA. I've even seen the words "reserve" and "winemaker's selection" used on four-litre bag-in-box wines that were barely fit to cook with.

WINE 4: MISTREATED WINE

WHAT TO LOOK FOR

wines that make an attribute of their oxidized flavours and brown colour, such as the incredibly unfashionable Madeira from Portugal

How times change. A century or two ago, Madeira was one of the world's most highly regarded wines, with people keeping the best vintages for decades, and paying big money for the privilege of drinking them when they were old. Today, the wine is all but completely unfashionable. It is made only on the tiny island of Madeira in the Atlantic Ocean, from very old-fashioned varieties such as Verdelho and Sercial. Always a strong, fortified wine, Madeira ranges from very dry (Sercial) to very sweet (Malmsey), but is always recognizable by its almost burnt, smoky flavours, its high, sometimes even slightly vinegary acidity, and its oxidized (literally, "maderized") smell – all of which are due to the fact that Madeira spends years, sometimes decades, sitting in old wooden barrels in hot warehouses.

Traditionally, it was considered to be even better if it had gone across the equator a couple of times in a wooden sailing ship, cooking even more. I know this doesn't sound very appealing, but believe me, good Madeira manages to rise above all these old-fashioned characters and is often a stunning drink.

WHEN THINGS GO WRONG

Not every wine is perfect. Things can, and do, go wrong all the time: in the vineyard, in the winery, and in the bottle. And these little disasters manifest themselves as faults: flavour and taste characteristics that spoil your enjoyment of a wine. What follows are a few of the main faults, so you can hopefully recognize them in the wines you drink – or, rather, don't drink:

♈ Cork taint. Caused by chemical compounds that can survive the sterilizing process of cork production, cork taint – when it's bad – is obvious to any nose as a musty, damp-cardboard type of smell. When it's there in low levels, it can take the edge off a wine, making it taste flat and dull. Estimates of how many cork-sealed wines are tainted run between two and ten per cent.

♈ Oxidation. If grape juice or wine comes into too much contact with oxygen, it oxidizes, turning the colour brown (in white or red wine), and leading to the wine smelling like sherry, or having aldehydic (unattractive, nutty) characters. Oxidation can also lead to...

♈ Volatile acidity. Characterized as the smell of vinegar or nail-polish remover, volatile acidity often makes itself known as a prickle in the nostrils, and makes a wine taste sharp. It is present in all wines in tiny amounts, and helps to lift the aroma, but if it's excessive, it can really mar your enjoyment.

♈ Sulphide. Sulphur is used in almost all grape-growing and winemaking, both as a fungicide and a preservative (for more on this, see "Going Back To Your Roots", page 134), and it can react with other chemicals – elements such as hydrogen, producing hydrogen sulphide – during fermentation. Again, a little sulphide character can give a wine an attractive mineral, smoke, and savoury quality. Too much hydrogen sulphide, though, and the wine can taste rubbery and smell like rotting eggs.

♈ Haziness. A little cloudiness is kind of OK in an unfiltered red wine (for more on this, see "Going Back To Your Roots", page 134), but too much haziness or a milky colour indicates that the wine may have suffered bacterial spoilage – something you'll soon pick up when you smell it. In contrast, powdery, crusty sediment in red wines and crunchy crystal deposits in white wines (particularly sweet whites) are harmless, and are simply tartaric acid which crystallizes over time if the wine gets cold.

It might be worth mentioning here that there is also a grey area involved when talking about faults, where one wine drinker's favourite character in a wine is another drinker's glaring fault. For instance, I might like a wine that, to me, tastes lifted and aromatic, but my drinking buddy might be reeling from what he describes as excessive volatile acidity: two ways of perceiving the same thing.

WINES YOUR GRANNY DRINK
Why are fortified wines so uncool?

You're feeling very smart tonight, very sharp. You've splurged on a new outfit, you're all spruced up, looking good, feeling a hundred per cent. You leave your brand-new inner-city warehouse loft-conversion apartment and walk a couple of blocks to your favourite bar, where the music is down-tempo loungey and the style is ultra-hip '80s retro. You take a seat, and can't help noticing that the very attractive bartender is there to take your order a little faster than usual. "So," says the bartender, suggestively, "what'll it be tonight?" You pause, stringing out the moment, then answer: "A nice glass of port, please."

And then you wake from your nightmare, drenched in sweat, trembling. *Port?!?* God! What were you *thinking*?

Let's face it: fortified wines – that is, wines with added alcohol, such as port and sherry – are not exactly the world's most fashionable drinks. When the mythical hordes of Generation X go out to party, are they drinking sherry? Not on your life. Vodka, rum and Coke, designer beers, little bottles of sparkling wine sucked up through straws, obscure South American cocktails: yes, yes, yes. But fortified wines? I don't think so. Fortified wines are what your grandparents drank, aren't they?

AND THE ANSWER IS...

Well, yes. And their grandparents before them, and so on, and so forth back across centuries. And that's why, I think, they're so incredibly untrendy: most fortified wines simply taste so old-fashioned. Most modern young wine drinkers are used to finding fresh, young, fruity flavours in their well-made, squeaky-clean wines. Give them a glass of sherry and they're confronted with smells of old barrels, bottle-age, nuttiness, savouriness, and oxidized characters: the smells and flavours of age.

In this sense, then, I could have put fortified wines into the "Altered States" chapter (page 116), because for many people they're so weird

and unusual that they're in danger of extinction. Oh, people are still drinking heaps of fortifieds across the world, but sales figures are not increasing; in fact, in many cases, they are declining.

It wasn't always like this. Once upon a time, a few hundred years ago, fortified wines were very fashionable indeed. In fact, in many countries, they were by far the most common drink.

WHAT FORTICATION DOES TO A WINE

The practice of fortifying wine by adding alcohol (brandy, for example, or neutral-flavoured spirit) developed as a practical way of making wines stronger and more stable – less likely to go off, in other words, as they sat in barrels during long journeys by ship from the wine-producing country to the wine-drinking country. Because they spent so long in barrel, these wines would often react with oxygen and take on nutty, savoury, oxidized (or "aldehydic") flavours, but because the added alcohol usually stopped them from going off completely, the otherwise unwelcome oxidized flavours turned into strangely attractive, complex characters.

Different grape varieties and conditions in different regions then led to the development of a wide variety of fortified wine styles, from the bone-dry, sea-spray-fresh tang of a pale, straw-coloured fine fino or manzanilla sherry from the chalky-white, sun-drenched vineyards of southern Spain, through the powerful, spirity depth of a purple vintage port from the steep vineyards of the Douro Valley in northern Portugal, to the treacle-like, raisined richness of the Muscats and Tokays of the hot, flat vineyards of Rutherglen in Australia.

And actually, when you describe them like that, these so-called old-fashioned wines sound rather delicious, don't they? Maybe they will come back into fashion after all; maybe there are signs that they already are. Certainly, the drop-dead groovy restaurants and bars in my neck of the woods seem to pride themselves on offering a few great sherries and ports and stickies by the glass. And by all reports, they're selling these wines, too. There's hope yet.

DRINKING IT

I wouldn't suggest for a second that you try all these wines at once – the average alcohol level is about eighteen per cent, significantly higher than the table wines you're probably more used to drinking, which come in around twelve to thirteen per cent. Try them slowly, one at a time. The extra alcohol hit is one of the reasons why sherry and port tend to be served and drunk in smaller glasses, but I would suggest you experiment with these wines in bigger, rounder glasses, and give the sometimes extraordinarily complex aromas a chance to blossom as you swirl.

WINE 1: DRY SHERRY

WHAT TO LOOK FOR

pale, bone-dry fino or manzanilla sherry, or off-dry amontillado sherry

Most sherry starts life as fairly dull, insipid, light white wine made from Palomino grapes, which has a little alcohol added to bring the total strength to about fifteen per cent. Old wooden barrels are then filled with the wine, but not completely, so there is some contact between the air and oxygen. In the part of Spain where sherry is made, a film of yeast called *flor* grows on the surface of the wine, protecting it from too much oxidation, stopping it from going brown, and contributing a tangy, yeasty flavour. The wine spends a number of years in barrel before being fortified a little more (to about 15.5 per cent), bottled, and sold. If the *flor* dies off (due to higher fortification, for example), the wine begins to darken in colour and take on a nuttier, slightly deeper flavour. This is called amontillado sherry.

DRINKING TIP: NOT JUST CAKE AND BISCUITS

Dry sherries are perfect drinks for the beginning of a meal. Their tangy, mouth-watering, savoury qualities not only serve to rev up the gastric juices, but they also work as the perfect partners for entrée-style, appetizer-type food: chilled glasses of fino with olives or prawns; cool (but not too cold) amontillado with translucent Spanish or Parma ham; that type of thing. Sweet fortifieds, on the other hand, are great to bring out at the end of the meal – it's a cliché, I know, but it works. Muscat matches sticky toffee pudding; vintage port and blue cheese marry well, as do sweet oloroso and a strong espresso coffee and bittersweet chocolate.

WINE 2: SWEET SHERRY

WHAT TO LOOK FOR

some oloroso sherries are sweeter than others (for sweet, look for the word *dulce* on the label), but the most commonly encountered sweet sherry is cream, and the most powerfully rich and sweet sherry is Pedro Ximénez ("PX")

If the light Palomino wine that goes into barrel has been fortified up to eighteen per cent so that no *flor* grows right from the beginning of the process, the eventual wine style is called oloroso: a dark, really intense, nutty, and dry sherry. Sweet sherries, such as the ubiquitous cream style, are usually olorosos that have been sweetened with concentrated grape juice. Pale cream sherries are usually fino sherries that have been sweetened, or oloroso-based cream sherries that have had the colour removed. The best (and therefore most expensive) sweet sherries are olorosos that are sweetened by the addition of the chocolatey-rich Pedro Ximénez, also known as "PX" or "black sherry". PX is, in itself, an amazing wine made from Pedro Ximénez grapes that have shrivelled and raisined in the sun before fermentation.

WINE 3: OLD PORT

WHAT TO LOOK FOR

port with the word "tawny" on the label – preferably also one that stipulates an average age – ten years old is good, twenty is much better, and anything older than that should be mind-blowing

We drank a vintage port all the way back in the "Firewater" chapter (page 40). The difference between vintage and tawny is how long the wine spends in barrel before being bottled. Vintage, you'll remember, is made from deep-coloured red grapes and is put into barrel as a deep-purple wine, coming out after only a couple of years to spend the rest of its life in bottle, like a table wine.

Tawny port, on the other hand, is left to mature in the barrels, sometimes for decades, during which time the deep-purple colour fades, turning tawny-brown, and the wine slowly reacts with oxygen, taking on nutty, woody, smoky, savoury smells, and moving from rich and tannic to more intense and fine. Good old tawny can be quite similar to good old sweeter oloroso sherry, with both styles exhibiting quite strong oxidized or *rancio* characters ("smelling like old walnut tables or treasure chests" is how I like to describe *rancio*).

WINE 4: FORTIFIED DESSERT WINES

EXAMPLES

Tokay, Liqueur Muscat
(Rutherglen, Australia)
Marsala (Sicily, Italy)
Málaga (Spain)
Jerepigo (South Africa)

Muscat grapes in the warm vineyards of Rutherglen can ripen to extremely high sugar levels, often with the grapes raisining on the vine. The sticky-sweet grapes are then crushed and pressed, and fermentation is initiated. After only two or three per cent of the sugar has been converted to alcohol, the wine is fortified up to about eighteen per cent and put into barrels, where it sits – like tawny port and sherry – for years and years, deepening in colour (the oldest Muscats are black-brown, like molasses, and coat the inside of a glass if you swirl them around). The finished wine that ends up in bottle is, like almost all non-vintage-dated fortified wine, a blend: some ten-year-old wine might be blended with a little thirty-year-old wine, to give it depth and complexity, and some three-year-old wine, to give it fruit flavour and freshness. The result is a tooth-achingly sweet, dark-mahogany, syrupy liquid with flavours of raisins, spice, toffee, and burnt marmalade.

THE *SOLERA* SYSTEM

As I said, most fortified wines you drink are blends of wines from different years, and the traditional way that these are blended is in something called the *solera* system. Imagine six barrels, one on top of the other, with the bottom barrel containing old wine, the top barrel young wine. Every time some wine is drawn from the bottom barrel for bottling, it is replaced by wine from the barrel above it – which is replaced by wine from the barrel above that, and so on until you get to the top barrel, which is topped up with the new vintage. You can see how, over a number of years, the wine in the bottom barrel would come to contain fractions of wine from many different years, and, consequently, becomes both complex and balanced, as the fuller wines from the warmer years balance out the leaner wines from the cooler years.

GOING BACK TO YOUR ROOTS
Organic and "natural" wines

Sometimes it feels as if the world has gone mad. Food scares, mad cow disease, images on the telly of burning pyres of livestock, fears over genetically modified foods, cloned monkeys, rampant globalization, rapidly advancing technology... it's as though all those apocalyptic stories we read in books and comics as kids are coming true. No wonder the whole push toward organic farming and toward slower, more natural ways of doing things, is gaining momentum. No wonder more people are looking for food – and for wines – they can trust.

Take a look at the shelves of your local wine shop or supermarket and you'll see an increasing number of bottles with words and phrases like "organic", "unfiltered", "old vine", "wild yeast", "minimal intervention" on the label – all indicating that the grape growers and winemakers involved in the production of these wines are consciously making an effort to do what they do in a sustainable, careful, natural way, close to the way that our ancestors made wine.

WHY GO ORGANIC?

Much of the motivation for these people is, of course, a concern for the environment and people's health and well-being. In some countries, large-scale broad-acre viticulture has had a major impact on the waterways and soil. The irrigation schemes along the huge Murray River in outback Australia, for example, have been essential to the establishment of that country's commercial wine industry, but they have also contributed to a dramatic rise in the levels of salinity in the soil. A consequence of such effects is a strong belief that less interference in the vineyard and winery – using fewer chemicals such as fungicides on the vines and preservatives in the wine, for example – produces healthier, more natural wines. And there is also a strong belief that adopting "natural" practices makes for better-tasting wine. Some winemakers argue, for instance, that fermenting with the wild, or ambient yeasts that are floating around in the vineyard rather than using cultured yeasts out of a packet produces more complexity and a better texture in the finished wine, and that using fewer chemicals allows the wine to more clearly express the flavour and taste characteristics derived from the terroir of the vineyard.

There's a nice parallel here with what's happening in popular music. After the techno-led revolution of the '80s, when everything seemed to be synthesized and electronic, you only have to look at the number of successful bands these days that have pared their sounds right back to the classic combination of guitar, drum, bass, and vocal. Look at the success of alternative roots music, too: world music, country, folk, and jazz are all increasingly appreciated.

THE PROBLEMS OF POLARIZATION

And just as fans of alternative roots music are passionate about their obsession and tend to be scornful of (or downright hostile toward) mass-culture mainstream music, so the supporters of alternative roots wines tend to be scathing in their condemnation of big-volume, commercially branded wines. These commercial wines, say the critics, are bland, characterless, and formulaic, and appeal to the lowest common denominator; in contrast, they feel that "real" wines or "artisan" wines, made in a particular place by passionate people, are wines with personality, soul, and a connection to the earth. Many others argue that the wine industry has to be polarized like this, with mass-production techniques and technology providing cheap wines for everyday drinking, and small-production techniques and real people hand-crafting wines for those who care a little more about what they put in their mouths.

But with such polarization comes tension: the little guys feeling squeezed out by the big guys, the big guys feeling the little guys are a waste of space. It's going to be interesting to see, over the next few years, which side will win out. What with the increasing rationalization takeovers and mergers in the industry, I know this flies in the face of logic, but my money, actually, is on the little guys. Eventually.

ORGANIC BIODYNAMI VIEILLES VIGNES UNFILTERED

DRINKING IT

Choosing wines as examples in this chapter was tricky, as almost all of the wines I've already talked about in the rest of the book come in "roots" versions. You can find Australian Shiraz, for example, that happens to be organic; Pinot Noir that happens to be unfiltered; Champagne made from old vines, etc. There are few or no examples of "roots" wines, in other words, that I haven't already talked about somewhere else in their "conventional" forms. So I've gone for general examples and talked more about the broader issues in each case – even some non-wine issues such as the precarious future of our planet.

WINE 1: ORGANIC WINE

WHAT TO LOOK FOR

organic wines are made all over the world in all different styles, but there are probably more organic wines (labelled *vin biologique*) in France than anywhere else

Growing grapes organically essentially means not using any synthetic chemicals, such as pesticides and fungicides, in the vineyard. Making wine organically also means not using synthetic additions and handling the wine as little as possible: only minimally filtering it, or not filtering it at all (*see* Wine 2). There is no reason at all why organic wine should taste any different to "conventional" wine; even less reason to expect it to look or taste murky or unattractively "funky". Also, strictly speaking, to legitimately call your wine organic, your vineyards and winemaking practices must be certified by one of the many regulatory bodies that police this area.

Controversially, a number of highly respected wine producers around the world choose to work outside this system, and although they follow organic principles in both vineyard and winery, choose not to seek certification – either for marketing or practical reasons. If, for instance, they simply have to spray the vines to eradicate unexpected pests, then they can, without losing any "official" organic status.

WINE 2: UNFILTERED WINE

WHAT TO LOOK FOR

it's becoming more and more common to find the word "unfiltered" proudly emblazoned on wine labels, indicating, not surprisingly, that the wine has been bottled without filtration

As you can imagine, before, during, and after fermentation, grape juice and wine is pretty murky stuff, full of fragments of grape skin, pulp, yeast, lees, and all sorts of bits and pieces that make their way in from the vineyard. Most of us like to drink clear, star-bright wine, so all wines are clarified before bottling. The first stage in clarification is fining: a protein or similar substance (egg whites are traditional, a kind of clay called bentonite is common) is added to the wine to take out the microscopic particles and make the wine stable. The second stage is filtering: literally passing the wine through a very fine filter or membrane to take out any solid particles such as yeast or lees. While fining is commonly practised (and acceptable in organic wines if an organic fining agent such as egg whites is used), filtering is sometimes avoided by letting the wine clarify itself over time by settling before bottling. The argument for this is that filtration takes richness, complexity, and flavour out of the wine.

ADDITIVES AND ALLERGIES

Almost all wine you drink has some form of preservative and/or antioxidant added to it in small quantities – a few dozen parts per million, for example. The most common are ascorbic acid (vitamin C) and sulphur dioxide, a common preservative found in many other processed foods (and in higher concentration, too). A small number of people (about two per cent of us) have allergic, often asthmatic reactions to sulphur dioxide. But many more complain of negative reactions such as headache or sinus pain when they drink wine. One explanation is that sufferers may be intolerant of substances in wine such as histamine-like biogenic amines, or the colour or tannin compounds, or (heaven forbid) alcohol. As a result, winemakers are using fewer preservatives, and, in a minority of cases, using none at all. Be careful, though, of wines labelled "preservative-free"; not surprisingly, these tend to oxidize quite quickly, so look for as recent a vintage as you can find.

WINE 3: OLD-VINE WINE

EXAMPLES

"old vine" Shiraz (Australia)

vieilles vignes red burgundy (France)

As I've said elsewhere in this book, the conventional wisdom is that the older a vine gets, the better the quality of wine produced from it should be: as the vine ages, the yield tends to drop, producing more concentrated flavours. The vine can live for centuries, but because most of the wine regions of the world (certainly in Europe) were ravaged by the vine louse known as phylloxera from the 1850s on, comparatively few vineyards contain vines that are more than a few decades old. Those vineyards that do, however – particularly in Australia, small pockets of France, the USA, and resurgent, very old areas of Spain and Italy – make the most of their heritage and are quick to tell you how ancient their vines are. In many cases, the hype is justified, with old-vine wines really showing more depth of flavour and interest. But be careful: no country regulates how old a vine has to be before it can claim ancient status, so there are some "old-vine" wines out there that stretch the boundaries of credibility when you taste them.

WILD AND CRAZY YEASTS!

Call them what you will: wild yeasts, ambient yeasts, natural yeasts, whatever. The point is that there is a difference between opening a packet of yeast that has been cultured in a laboratory, and relying, as *vignerons* have done for millennia, on the yeasts floating in the air, settled on grape skins, and sitting inside the fermenting vat to start fermentation. Many winemakers – particularly in New World wine countries where adding cultured yeast is the norm – are moving back to wild yeasts as a way of making (hopefully) more complex wines. There is also an argument that using yeasts indigenous to the place where the wine is made is another form of expressing that place's terroir, or "somewhereness".

WINE 4: BIODYNAMIC WINE

WHAT TO LOOK FOR

harder to find than organic wines, biodynamic wines (*biodynamie* in French) almost always display the symbol of the biodynamic association that has certified them

Biodynamics is like a far more rigorous and mystical version of organics, with extreme emphasis on practices designed to "dynamize" the soil. As well as forbidding any kind of synthetic chemicals in the vineyard, the biodynamic *vigneron* will add "preparations" to the vineyard (mixtures of composted herbs, leaves, and other prescribed ingredients) in accordance with phases of the moon and the stars. While it's easy to be sceptical, a number of the best wine producers in France and some other parts of the world have moved to biodynamics and claim that it has made a difference to the quality of their wines.

As with all roots winemaking, because the *vigneron* is relying less on remedial treatment and more on natural influences, it is even more important that the right (most appropriate) grape variety be planted on the vineyard site, and that the winemaker pays more careful attention to the detail of the whole process – two factors that in themselves can increase quality.

INDEX